RESOURCES FOR TEACHING

Critical Strategies
for Academic Thinking
and Writing

A TEXT AND READER

SECOND EDITION

Prepared by

BARBARA GROSS
Rutgers University — Newark

with

MALCOLM KINIRY
Rutgers University — Newark

MIKE ROSE
University of California,
Los Angeles

Bedford Books *of* St. Martin's Press   •   Boston

For information, write: St. Martin's Press, Inc.
175 Fifth Avenue, New York, NY 10010

Editorial Offices: Bedford Books *of* St. Martin's Press
29 Winchester Street, Boston, MA 02116

ISBN: 0–312–06642–2

Preface

The comments that follow are meant to encourage instructors to make *Critical Strategies for Academic Thinking and Writing* their own, to draw connections and make assignments that fit the needs of their students.

We begin with an introduction that discusses some ways to use *Critical Strategies*, including a section designated for new teachers but helpful, too, to instructors who have not used this text before. We then proceed through Part One, demonstrating several ways to approach the three-part structure of each chapter — the introductory materials, the First Passes, and the Options. For each chapter, we suggest ways to approach the assignments and strategies for class discussions, as well as connections among the readings. The manual includes suggestions for a variety of writing tasks and classroom activities that underscore the importance of active reading, critical thinking, and engaged writing.

We want to encourage students to view these strategies as choices that put them at the center of their own learning, as ways to think critically about the range of academic materials they encounter here and in their other courses. Therefore, we emphasize the importance of using the strategies to develop interpretive perspectives, and we underscore that these ways of thinking do not exist in isolation from one another. We point out ways to move recursively through the materials, emphasizing connections among themes, readings, and ways of thinking about the issues.

Each of the chapters in Part Two asks students to focus on a single topic and to employ their critical thinking strategies as they perform various research tasks. We discuss the readings individually and recommend ways to group them, including shortened versions of the chapters for instructors whose course allows time for only a limited number of readings.

Our intent throughout is to provide you and your students with choices, with a range of materials and assignments that encourage students to think critically about what they read and about the strategies that are available to them as they learn and as they communicate what they know to others.

Contents

Contents

Contents

General Introduction

We intend *Critical Strategies for Academic Thinking and Writing* to contribute to a writing class in which students are reading, discussing, and critiquing a variety of materials from a range of disciplines and writing about them — both in short, exploratory journal entries and papers as well as in longer, more structured essays. In such a class, students are encouraged to reflect on their thinking and writing and to push beyond traditional academic topics — to use their writing to take intellectual chances, to push continually at the boundaries of what they know.

Sequencing and the Use of Classroom Time

Although we have thought hard about issues of sequencing, we are not bound, and do not want to bind others, to a single way of moving through this book. We do believe the book invites instructors to think critically about issues of sequencing: How do we structure writing classes and writing assignments in cumulatively powerful and instructive ways?

Our own preference is for a recursive approach. We think that students gain confidence as writers when they find themselves building, trying out, and reusing a strategic repertory to meet a variety of reading and writing problems. The chapters into which this book divides — defining, summarizing, serializing, classifying, comparing, and analyzing — are offered as testing grounds for such a repertory. The best ways to move among the book's materials are ways that enable students to take advantage in a new setting of something they've tried out in another.

The table of contents of *Critical Strategies* can mislead, for it seems to offer a pattern of discrete modes in linear progression: First we master defining, then we move on to serializing; eventually we'll work on comparisons before taking on analysis: Except for exam situations, relatively few academic assignments call for these strategies in isolation. Thus you'll notice from the outset that definition problems lend themselves to comparing strategies, that a good way to handle a serializing assignment is to establish an analytical perspective, and so on. We try to suggest such interrelation in the text.

Related to the issue of sequencing is another practical classroom concern: how to make the best use of time. This concern gives rise to two contradictory anxieties: (1) How do I fill the time available? What if my plan doesn't hold, and the class starts to go flat? (2) How do I economize? How do I make fullest use of the time available to me? How do I avoid wasting time?

Perhaps we exaggerate by calling these feelings contradictory, for they express the same desire: How do I make my classes rich and helpful experiences for students? But they come from opposite apprehensions: "I'll never find enough to do" versus "I'll never find a way to get this all done." We hope that the format of *Critical Strategies* allows you to minimize both anxieties. Working with short readings and relatively discrete problems gives you the latitude of moving on when something feels done or when you and your students are not getting anywhere. Both the First Passes and the Options, when treated as classroom exercises, give you the ability to find your own rhythm as you go. You can lighten yourself of the burden of overplanning. Working within an easier rhythm of talk–write–talk, you can afford to plan more open-endedly: See what people have to say about, for example, Linda Hogan's "Death, Etc." (p. 259) or Barbara Tomlinson's list of metaphors about composing (p. 163), then open the class to further discussion, culminating, if the discussion warrants, in a short homework assignment that asks for a journal entry or a short essay.

See what students have to say about any one reading, then open the class to further discussion or a add another reading, culminating, if the discussion warrants, in a homework assignment that asks for a journal entry or a short essay. Or ask students to do and think about another reading as a homework assignment. These discussions can move within chapters or, if you prefer, can cross back and forth among two or more chapters, making thematic connections or asking students to look back at strategies they have used earlier in the course.

Using a Journal

Journals work well with this book. Since so many assignments suggest short, improvisational work, it's a good idea to formalize this component of your course by asking students to preserve their writing. Although instructors will use journals in various ways, we recommend reader–response journals in which students try out approaches to assignments, write about their reactions to readings, and consider their difficulties as they encounter specific materials. Journals also provide a fine opportunity for students to examine the strategies by which they learn and by which they communicate what they know.

As students keep journals, they may feel as if they're rather randomly collecting bits and pieces of information, ideas, and observations. You may want to point out that although this process feels fragmented, it is, in fact, the way knowledge is gained and research is done. If you ask students to think about their own history as learners, they may come to realize that their own learning has not happened in a simple linear pattern but has been cumulative and recursive. You might profitably spend part of a class discussing this personal learning history.

And a brief discussion of how knowledge is gained in any field will reinforce the point. The Morse essay in "Summarizing," for example, demonstrates that knowledge and understanding do not happen in a linear pattern; both result from using a variety of thinking strategies and collecting ideas and information over time until the picture becomes more and more complete.

Students should be encouraged to look at their journals repeatedly during the course and to make connections whenever they can. Devoting class time to this process of reflection can enhance the work of the course and reaffirm the notion that the strategies students are working with do not exist in isolation but are interrelated processes of coming to know the world.

Other Practical Matters

Here we'll simply offer a list:

The introductory sections of chapters work best if read interactively. Each embeds several exercises in the discussion. You might want to ask students to spend a few minutes writing and then to discuss their ideas. Having tried to write a bit about a particular problem, students are better equipped to participate in and to read discussion of that problem.

The book lends itself to spin–off assignments. The opportunities for these may occur unpredictably as individual students respond to particular readings. Some assignments might lead to short research projects; some may connect to readings in other chapters of the book. We've suggested some possibilities for this kind of connection and expansion within this manual. And when you find your students critically engaged with the materials, we recommend looking for ways to let them pursue their interests.

In a number of assignments in each chapter, we invite personal essays — opportunities to draw on life experiences in relation to academic readings. These assignments won't present the same opportunities for everyone, nor will we have anticipated all the opportunities. Here, too, we recommend flexibility, encouraging students to let their own stories emerge as opportunities present themselves.

Throughout the book, and particularly in the First Passes section of each chapter, we ask students to reflect not only on the materials themselves but also on their own thinking processes. These proddings will not always produce excellent writing, but they do encourage students to stand back a bit and to examine their own intellectual efforts.

The distinctions between First Passes and Options are somewhat arbitrary. Often assignments called First Passes have lent themselves to extended writing; conversely, the Options sometimes work well when handled only briefly. In general, though, the Options require more reading and will probably take up more class time.

The chapters in Part Two also contain materials that can be drawn on along the way. There is no reason why these chapters should be treated as a world apart or as something students can only build toward gradually. In fact, we suggest ways to use the last two chapters throughout the course, as a central feature of your work with each of the chapters in Part One.

Thinking about Course Plans

This text is designed to be a rich collection of materials from which instructors and students can draw according to the needs of the class and the interests of the individual instructor. The text presents more than any class could do in a semester, so there's room to move around, to pick and choose, to emphasize different skills. We offer here only a few of the many possibilities for organizing a semester's work.

A Linear Approach. You could, of course, move through the chapters one by one, asking students to work on the First Passes in each chapter and to write an essay based on their or your choice of Options. The First Passes can be done in class — and many of the writing assignments can be rough and exploratory. You may choose to assign one finished product at the end of each chapter or to combine assignments to encompass more than one chapter at a time. And you might choose one or two of the chapters in Part Two for the class to work on together, or you might allow individual students or small groups to choose a chapter to work on. This work could culminate in a final paper and/or a report to the class (perhaps with several days at the end of the semester devoted to research forum type presentations). To avoid the impression that each of the first six chapters stands alone and results in a particular "type" of essay, you might emphasize during the work with the final chapters how the thinking strategies students have been working with one at a time interact and support one another.

A Circular Approach. In another approach, you might proceed more quickly (perhaps one week per chapter) through each of the strategies in Part One, perhaps focusing only on the First Passes, and then using the second half of the course to work on one or more of the chapters in Part Two, as a way of bringing together and reviewing the strategies used in Part One. Or your could move through the First Passes and then return to the Options during the second half of the course, incorporating excursions into the materials of Part Two whenever they're relevant. (For example, when you work with "Analyzing," you could substitute one essay and one piece of fiction from the Caribbean fiction chapter for the Options included at the end of Chapter 6.) If you choose this approach, you can vary the pace of the writing by asking students to mix less formal writing with longer essays.

A Selective Approach. You might instead select just a few chapters in Part One and focus on those, leaving time for work with two or more chapters in Part Two during the second half of your course. You could build a course around "Summarizing," "Classifying," "Comparing," and "Analyzing," for example, and then move into "Women and Power" and "Caribbean Fiction" to give students the experience of using these strategies with two rather different types of material. Or you could begin with "Defining," "Summarizing," "Comparing," and "Analyzing," and then move to "Apes and Language" and "The Causes and Treatments of Schizophrenia." Many such combinations are possible; any one you select should give your students a rich experience in this course and many skills that will help as they approach other courses as well.

A Sourcebook Approach. Another alternative begins with one of the chapters in Part Two. You might, for example, focus on Chapter 7, "Women and Power," and have students tackle one of the more ambitious essays suggested in that chapter. By asking students to attempt such a project early on, subject to later revisions, you set up an arena for bringing the various strategies to bear upon a project already under way. The need for defining, the advantages of comparing, the usefulness of summary, these become part of the work in progress. After working with one chapter (7, 8, 9, and 10 work well here), the course moves back to whichever of the earlier chapters you see as most relevant to the work your students are doing. This approach lends itself well to teaching revision — and to using Nancy Sommers' article about revising strategies of beginning college writers and experience writers. You might also want to use a portfolio system, in which all the term's work is resubmitted at the end of the semester.

A Research Approach. Yet another possibility involves beginning with one of the research chapters. Chapter 12 might work well here because it engages students in understanding their intended major or the institution they're attending. Chapter 11 provides a different but also easily workable focal point. If you choose this approach, you might review the beginning of the chapter with your students early in the semester so they can begin gathering data. Then you can select chapters in Part One — or work through the First Passes of each chapter — and relate each to the ongoing research students are conducting. The manual sections on these chapters include more specific suggestions for a course plan organized this way.

While it is possible to build a syllabus on the thematic connections among materials in this text, you will probably want to use those connections more improvisationally in your work with Part One. Perhaps their best uses occur in the midst of particular assignments, when you can refer students to related readings or draw on their work with an earlier chapter. When they can combine several strategies this way, you underscore the value of a flexible repertory of thinking and writing strategies. Such side trips and exploratory journeys are, therefore, very much in the spirit of the book.

We offer here a short list of thematically grouped readings in Part One; the manual chapters suggest additional connections, and we're sure you and your students will come up with many others as well.

Alienation: How do social and personal circumstances distance us from others and from ourselves?

Wallace and Waters and Martin E. P. Seligman's Theory of Help-lessness, p. 295

Redfield, "Little Communities," p. 184

Kingston, "From *The Woman Warrior*," p. 306

Punk Rock ("Analyzing": A Sociology Option), p. 313

Terkel, "Roberto Acuña," p. 75

Moral and Social Implications of Science

Howard and Rifkin, "Eugenics in America," p. 46

Singer, "Defining Ethics," p. 52

Steinfels, Thomas, Comparing Arguments, p. 240

Evaluating Multiple Perspectives — "Analyzing," p. 297

Keller, Goodfield, A Science Option, p. 319

Whether you ask your students to move among these materials in a linear way or in a more circular pattern — or perhaps in a series of exploratory forays whose results you can't anticipate — we hope you will find the assignments and readings ample enough, varied enough, and problematic enough to sustain your students' interest and invite their critical thinking.

To New Teachers

We think of *Critical Strategies for Academic Thinking and Writing* as a sourcebook of materials from which you can draw a range of assignments, depending on your interests, the abilities and backgrounds of your students, and the departmental and institutional contexts in which you teach. As we've talked to teachers who have used the book, however — especially teachers who are new to the composition classroom — we've come to think that some orientation on ways to use the readings, to sequence assignments, and to engage students in difficult academic material would be helpful.

This introduction begins with some general comments on the structure of *Critical Strategies* and the readings it comprises. We then discuss more specifically how to use the book. For Part One we suggest some ways to sequence assignments and use the chapter introductions, First Passes, and Options. For Part Two we suggest ways to prepare students for and guide them through the hefty amount of reading they encounter in the first four chapters of the part and the research demands of the final two chapters. We conclude with some thoughts on stimulating classroom discussion, responding to student writing, and creating an intellectually rigorous but supportive classroom atmosphere. As often as possible, we draw on specific examples of how we've used this book in class, and the results we've gotten from our students. However much or little our students resemble yours, we hope that these glances into our classrooms will offer you some insight into using this book effectively in your own.

About This Book

Each of the six chapters in Part One of *Critical Strategies* has a three-part structure. The chapter introduction, called Working with the Strategy, poses an opening problem and then illustrates the chapter's guiding strategy at work in varied academic situations. The second section, called First Passes, suggests short assignments for which students are encouraged to draft brief, provisional responses, opening the way to classroom discussion, collaborations with classmates, and revisions. Each chapter ends with a number of Options, full-fledged writing assignments based on representative academic readings.

There are two kinds of chapters in Part Two, both with a two-part structure. Each begins in Framing the Issues with a set of preliminary readings to which students are asked to respond. Then, in the section called Complicating the Issues students will find readings that modify, support, dispute, or deepen the initial readings. Each chapter is designed to work as a minilibrary, but without some of the frustrations that come with library research. In the final two chapters, students are asked to conduct their own investigations; there the Framing the Issues sections offer suggestions for doing field research. Students can work solely with the data they collect, or they can draw from a series of brief theoretical or research-based readings printed in the book.

The Structure of This Book

There are a number of effective paths you can chart through this book, depending on your own pedagogy and the needs of your students. The simplest, of course, is to follow the book linearly, chapter by chapter. Another is to begin with an overview of selected strategies and then return to them for more intensive work. Yet another is to begin with a complex problem drawn from the material in Part Two and then systematically bring the strategies in Part One to bear on it.

A number of new teachers have told us that, at least for their first time using the book, they would prefer to have some guidance on the most "direct" or "straightforward" or "uncomplicated" way to use *Critical Strategies*. If you find yourself in that position, we offer the following suggestions:

— Begin with "Defining" or "Summarizing" and, following the order in the table of contents, select the strategies that seem most important and that you can fit into your time frame. *It takes about one and a half to two weeks to do justice to a given strategy.*

— When we have taught a so-called remedial course in a ten-week quarter, we have used "Defining," "Summarizing," "Serializing," "Comparing," and "Analyzing." In regular composition, we have used "Defining," "Summarizing," "Classifying," and "Comparing" (which we combined), and "Analyzing," and had students select a chapter in Part Two. The semester system allows you to include more and provide fuller treatment.

— Even if you do not assign the chapter introductions in Part One, consider using the opening problems. Do these in class, then assign at least one or two of the First Passes — students can start these in class and complete them there or at home. (Treat some of these opening problems and First Passes as warm-ups; not all of them have to result in polished papers.) If time permits, cover one or more Options.

— If you plan to use Part Two, it is wise to make that assignment fairly early in the term, even though you probably won't get to it formally until later. Students who select "Women and Power," "Caribbean Fiction," "The Causes and Treatments of Schizophrenia," or "Apes and Language" will need to begin the reading early. (A two-page progress report at some point in the term will ensure that students are doing the reading and will assist them.) Students who select "What's Funny?" or "Exploring the Discourse of Your Major" will need to begin early because those chapters require field research. (Again, a brief progress report is a good idea.)

The Readings in *Critical Strategies*

We selected and edited the readings in *Critical Strategies* with the intention of helping students develop the ability to write about academic material. To assure a fairly representative selection, we surveyed syllabi, textbooks, and anthologized materials from a wide range of lower-division courses in humanities and social sciences and, to a somewhat lesser degree, in fine arts and physical sciences at the University of California and at selected state and community colleges in California. Over the years of development of *Critical Strategies,* we compared our findings with materials gathered from other schools in other states. The readings in this volume, then, are similar in kind to the readings students will encounter through their first few years in college. In our experience, working with these materials will help students considerably as they move through their lower-division curriculum.

Working with readings in this way may seem unusual for a composition textbook, for traditionally such textbooks provide readings as models of effective prose or as illustrations of rhetorical strategies. Certainly some of the readings in *Critical Strategies* could be used in that way: Quite a few are fine pieces that could be appreciated and imitated or analyzed. But more often the assignments we offer require students to take a reading apart, use sections of it, puzzle, even fret over it. And in those cases when the authors' prose is difficult or ungraceful, when they could have organized a piece more effectively or said things more clearly — all that becomes part of what students must learn to work with as they become increasingly adept at using primary and secondary sources to develop their own writing.

We have tried to use readings that raise central academic themes (for example, social versus biological influences on behavior) and tasks (for example, interpreting data and critiquing theoretical perspectives). At the same time, we've tried to select readings that are interesting in some way, or that relate directly to students' lives — like the readings about pop culture, immigration, and gender roles. But even the most carefully chosen academic materials will feature the weaknesses of academic prose as well as its strengths. Some are well written, others are not; some we could present in their entirety, others we had to edit to make accessible; the structure and topic of some will be more or less familiar to students, others will seem distant and opaque.

Because a fair number of the readings will, at first, be unfamiliar or difficult or will need some contextualizing, we find it helpful to provide students with a brief orientation to them. Frequently we set the scene or offer a few words on the structure of a piece, a little advance help with a difficult section of text, some advice on what to look for, or a few words of assurance and direction for an assignment that is unlike anything students have done before. Such information might come from our own reading of the material, or from the instructor's manual, or even from the headnote in the textbook — calling attention to it, elaborating on it. Let us give a few examples.

This is from the Education Option in Chapter 5, "Comparing" (pp. 247–255). In this assignment, students are asked to compare a section from Benjamin Franklin's *Autobiography* with an excerpt from *The Autobiography of Malcolm X*, both of which have to do with learning to read and write, though in very different historical and social circumstances. The passage by Malcolm X contains some specific references that most students will find unfamiliar, but it is powerfully direct and should not present any major problems of comprehension. The excerpt from Franklin's *Autobiography*, however, is more difficult. We provide some assistance with it when making the assignment.

Here are some ideas. A brief summary of the reading, just a few sentences to give the students a general idea of what the piece is about, is a useful start. It is also helpful to say something about the arcane language and allusions, assuring students that it's ok to read something through once to get the general idea and not worry about words that seem strange. Another way to provide this general orientation to the reading is to point out, without comment, a few key phrases: "Often I sat up in my room reading the greater part of the night. . . .," "prose writing has been of great use to me in my life, and was a principal means of my advancement . . .," "We sometimes disputed, and very fond we were of argument. . . . ," "I thought the writing excellent, and wished, if possible, to imitate it." Yet another way to go is this: Since the various imitation exercises Franklin performed to improve his writing are important but difficult to follow, you could guide students through the last long paragraph, in which he describes those exercises. Teachers familiar with Franklin and his era could use a different approach to prepare students for the passage, telling them a bit about Franklin's personal philosophy and its influence on the American ethos — not a lecture, but just enough to sketch the historical context. (You would then want to do the same for Malcolm X.) There is more you can have students do — relating Franklin's experience to their own, for example — but these brief techniques will get them started with the reading.

For readings like this, what you decide to tell the class will be based on your own background, the level of the class, and the work they've done so far. But some preparation does seem helpful and enables you to move more quickly to the use of the materials for writing.

Some assignments are difficult not because the reading is abstract or needs to be placed in context, but rather because the readings are being used in unfamiliar ways. The Literature Option in the "Classifying" chapter, "Selected Opening Paragraphs from Works of Nonfiction," is a good example. Here students are given a number of introductory paragraphs from nonfiction, with these instructions:

> Read them, making notes on differences in style, person, tone, or
> any other characteristic that interests you. Then, as a way to
> consider the various strategies writers can use to open their work,
> experiment with different ways to classify these paragraphs.

Many students have never been asked to examine prose in this manner (as Richard Lanham would say, looking *at* it rather than *through* it), and this might be the first time they must consider a reading rhetorically, in terms of strategy. You may therefore need to say a few words about analyzing prose this way, possibly modeling the analysis of a few introductory paragraphs.

Some new teachers worry that a number of the readings involve disciplines unfamiliar to them: biological science, astronomy, economics — or, closer to home but still not their own neighborhood, sociology, political theory, and so on. The fundamental issues here are authority and expertise, sensitive issues for academics. We, too, felt pretty unsure of ourselves, even a little fraudulent, the first time we walked into a classroom with readings like James Trefil's "The End of The Universe" or the materials on nutrition in the "Analyzing" chapter. But we soon discovered the following:

— Our purpose is not to cover a body of material in the way an
astronomer or nutritional scientist would. Comprehensive treatment
is not the goal; the goal is facilitating sufficient comprehension to
enable students to write.

— We possessed more background knowledge in physical, biological,
and social science than we thought, and that helped us more than
we could have expected in guiding class discussion and in responding to papers.

— There was absolutely nothing demoralizing — to us or to the
students — about admitting that we were having trouble with a
section of reading. (Trefil, for example, relies on a number of
metaphors to help the reader comprehend the ways the universe

might end. Most are helpful, but one having to do with "a film being run at uniform speed . . . [and imagining] that the film speed is multiplied by ten when the power of ten goes up one digit" still makes our eyes cross.) In fact, it can be extremely helpful to your students for you to admit something throws you and to model how you continue to make sense of a reading in spite of a less-than-perfect understanding.

— Especially where the sciences are concerned, you might have some students in your class who can assist as expert guides. Rely on their knowledge, both in class discussion and in groups — maybe forming the groups to take advantage of their expertise.

Critical Strategies in the Classroom

Sequencing Assignments

It is important to give thought not just to individual assignments but to assignments across time — so that students can apply to new situations the techniques they have previously learned. Our illustration comes from the "Summarizing" chapter.

One "Summarizing" assignment we like, given the schools we've worked in, is the History Option on immigration laws. Students are provided a list of laws regulating immigration into the United States (taken primarily from Linda Perrin's *Coming to America)* — from the Alien Act of 1798 to the 1984 Simpson-Mazzoli Act, and they are asked to summarize the entries, describing the main historical trends in the U.S. immigration policy through 1984.

We would typically lead into this assignment with several easier assignments, done both in class and at home. One of the sequences of assignments we have used begins with the opening problem (the excerpt on schooling and nostalgia by Sara Lawrence Lightfoot), which introduces the strategy of summarizing, and moves on to First Pass #2 (a table showing the overall changes in regional distribution of world trade from 1876–1960), which requires students to consider and summarize historical and economic trends in broad numerical data. (We sometimes combine this with the table on p. 124, "Women in the Civilian Labor Force, 1890–1979.") These are done in class in a writing workshop format. Then we move to a different kind of text, a personal account from Studs Terkel's *Working,* the story of a farm worker and labor organizer, Roberto Acuña. To spark student discussion we pose the question: "Why does Acuña tell his story?" and build from that to a take-home assignment one or two paragraphs in length: "Write a summary of Roberto Acuña's account of his life, using as a guide the central idea you think he's trying to convey to his listeners/readers." (If students are having a hard time with this, we provide further structure with a sentence they can later discard: "Roberto Acuña's story is the story of a person's _____."

This sequence gives students a chance to develop some familiarity with a range of summarizing skills: abstracting and compressing a series of events, finding trends in numerical-historical data, selecting key events from a narrative to formulate a shorter, illustrative narrative. And the sequence, we've found, leads nicely to the assignment on immigration laws.

Another preparation for the immigration laws assignment is to have students make notes on trends they see as they read the list: chronological patterns, trends in the kinds of people or skills or geographical location most frequently restricted or encouraged, the role of general historical events (like the industrial revolution and wars) in shaping trends. When they come to class, then, they are primed for discussion. With assignments like these, we find it useful to begin by having students form groups of two or three to address the questions: What trends do you see? Can you come up with any reasons to help explain them? Once we get a sense that the groups have done their work (this can take from fifteen to twenty minutes), we ask volunteers to report their conclusions to the class. The reports generate further discussion that we try to direct toward the writing the students will be doing. We ask questions like, "Can you think of a way to express in a sentence or two this trend you're seeing — take a moment to do that" and "How would you support or illustrate that trend — what phrases from the text can you use for support?" Then we ask the class to help us draft an opening sentence for the paper, one students would be free to use if they need to. If everyone gets stuck, we suggest a sentence like: "When we examine the history of immigration laws in the United States from 1798 to 1984, certain trends emerge: _____, _____, and _____." We use this sentence, of course, to get people writing: They are free to drop it later, modify it, or reject it.

Because we have worked in schools with substantial recent immigrant populations, we like to add a section to this assignment. We ask students to conclude their summary of trends in the U.S. immigration laws by positioning their own histories, or their parents' histories, in relation to this longer history they've just recounted. These personal histories tend to emerge, in some form, during class discussion, and weaving the students' personal observations into the investigation of immigration laws helps make that history real and helps nonimmigrant students understand the human dimension of immigration legislation. If the majority of your students are not recent immigrants, but you'd like to do more with this assignment, then you can have the class interview their parents, relatives, or neighbors about their families' immigration histories, with an eye to matching those histories with the historical trends evident in the list of immigration laws.

Chapter Introductions

The chapter introductions in Part One begin with a problem that encourages students to think strategically from the start. Then comes a brief discussion that tries to set the academic context in which the particular strategy might prove useful. Finally there is the presentation of Cases, extended illustrations of the strategy at work. We encourage you to use these introductions in the same adaptive, creative ways we encourage you to use the assignments and readings in the balance of the book. Let us run through some possibilities.

Some teachers don't assign the chapter introductions at all, but read them to help shape their own approach to the strategy and to provide an illustration or two to present in class discussion.

Other teachers assign problems and cases selectively, but don't use the majority of the written text. For example, you could begin treatment of any of the chapters in Part One by having students, at home or in class, tackle the problem that opens the chapter. The directions provided for the students are pretty straightforward, though you might briefly review the "cues" and the questions listed under "Thinking about Thinking" and suggest that they keep a record of their thinking with some notes, however rough.

You might want to draw from some of the more immediately accessible cases as introductory passes at using the strategies. You could use the text surrounding the cases or simply the cases themselves, supplying your own context. Another way to provide this introductory pass — if you have time — is to have students, individually or in small groups, select a case based on their interests and majors.

Some teachers use the chapter introductions not only to initiate students to the use of a strategy, but also as a source of supplementary material while they're teaching the strategy. One teacher we know taught the "Serializing" chapter by starting with the opening problem, on the hydrologic cycle, and then using the poem "And Your Soul Shall Dance" and surrounding text to prepare students for a formal out-of-class paper on Jim Daniels's "Digger Goes on Vacation" (one of the First Passes). This teacher had her students read the whole introduction when they began the serializing strategy, then returned systematically to sections of it. It would also be feasible to have students simply read sections of the chapter introduction as those sections became pertinent to particular assignments.

And, of course, a teacher could assign a chapter introduction in a traditional manner, requiring students to read it by the time they begin working on the strategy. A word of advice here: We suggest that you provide some sort of orientation to the introduction, however brief. You might also ask students to formulate one question about the strategy that comes to mind after they've read the introduction.

Assignments

The menu of assignments in each chapter in Part One is divided into First Passes and Options. There are three First Passes in each chapter and five or six Options. We recommend that, time permitting, you have your class do at least two of the First Passes and then one or more of the Options, which tend to be a bit more difficult and require more work. The directions for First Passes are fuller and provide more suggestions than do those for the Options, and while either can lead to out-of-class papers, First Passes lend themselves more to in-class work, to trial runs, rehearsals, drafts that need not be extensively revised and polished.

First Passes.   Here's an example of working with an assignment under First Passes, this drawn from the Analyzing chapter.

The fundamental intellectual task that students have to master in "Analyzing" is the appropriation of a theoretical perspective. Students typically encounter several problems when first working with this strategy:

— Initial difficulty understanding the process itself, that the perspective is to be adopted and used to investigate and interpret

— Trouble seeing the perspective as one of many possible perspectives versus the "truth," the one right way

— Trouble establishing a critique of the perspectives they've taken on, turning the critical lens back on the perspective itself

— Failure to see the connection between the analytical process in *Critical Strategies* and the ongoing analytical activity in their day-to-day lives

You can anticipate problems like these when assigning a First Pass in "Analyzing," for example First Pass #2, Chapter 6, in which students read a newspaper account, "Gunman Kills Himself after Hostage Drama," and are asked to apply the psychologist Martin Seligman's perspective on competence and helplessness to the case of the gunman. Take the newspaper story first, asking students to summarize what happened. Students will have an easy time with this, recounting the details of the young gunman's hostage-taking and eventual suicide. If, in fact, this is the first "Analyzing" assignment you do, you might want to stay with the story a bit longer, forestalling the move to the perspective by Seligman. Ask, "Why do you suppose the gunman did what he did?" (In summarizing the newspaper story, students might already have offered observations about the gunman's motivation; if so, build on these.) Students usually get pretty lively here, offering a range of opinions. Here are some, tape recorded from a recent class discussion:

"He's crazy."

"He's really depressed. He's got this awful disease, and he's been seeing a psychiatrist for years."

"He's a loser, and he's doing this because he wants attention and a little recognition."

"He's not necessarily an evil guy; he's just really confused and desperate."

"It has to do with his mother . . . look at what she says, she says 'she's thankful no one else was hurt' . . . not 'Oh, my poor son,' or something like that."

"He's kinda like that guy Robert DeNiro plays in *Awakenings*. . . he just doesn't have any control over himself."

These opinions were coming pretty quickly, one student picking up where another left off, qualifying, amending, flat-out disagreeing. The teacher encouraged this exchange, then observed: "It's interesting how many possible explanations you've come up with, ranging from medical to psychological to environmental reasons for the gunman to be doing what he's doing. What I want us to reflect on is the way all of these explanations reveal theories of behavior. Every day we read stories like this one, and we always try to explain them to ourselves. We come up with a theory, an explanation, a perspective on the event. Let's talk for a moment about how the things you were saying reveal theories about behavior." The discussion continued, then the teacher said, "OK. You've offered a variety of theories. Let's take a look now at yet another theory — one, by the way, that shares some of the elements of some of the theories you've suggested." With this, the teacher turned to the passage from Martin Seligman's *Helplessness: On Depression, Development, and Death.*

To prepare students for this moderately difficult passage, you can provide the kind of assistance discussed in the section on reading. Also, it would be valuable to try to make the abstractions come alive. In the tape-recorded class, the teacher asked questions like these as the class worked its way through the Seligman piece: "Take a moment and think of a time in your life when you were afraid, and of a time when you were depressed. Did they feel different? What's the difference?" "Can you remember a time when you felt that the events of your life were not in your control?" "Think of a time when you were able to do well with a situation that could have caused you some pain or trouble. How did you feel afterward?" The teacher asked the students to write a few notes to themselves in response to the questions, and then asked volunteers to share their observations with the class, drawing connections, when they could, with the tenets of Seligman's theory.

The next step is the analytical move itself, using Seligman to inform an analysis of "Gunman Kills Himself after Hostage Drama." Some students will have been anticipating this move in various ways, but now it's explicit and can become the focus of discussion. In our experience, students do well with this, readily interpreting the hostage-taker's actions in terms of helplessness, depression, and the need for even a momentary sense of control. Once they've discussed and adopted Seligman, though, it is sometimes a little difficult to get them to assess the merits of his theory in relation to the gunman's story. We sometimes use metaphors like "trying on different kinds of lenses" or "stepping inside and outside" or "a movie camera's shifting point of view" to underscore the perspectival nature of analysis. To spark critical perspective, we sometimes break students into groups and pose questions like "Imagine you're using Seligman's theory to explain the gunman's actions to the hostage. What might she say in return?" Or we have them go back through the newspaper account and make a list of any information that was excluded as they developed their Seligman-based analysis of the gunman's behavior. Or we ask them if anyone is studying a theory of human behavior in any other class that might be useful here. Or we point out that, as a psychologist, Seligman is interested in individual, psychological explanations for why people do what they do, and we ask our students to draw on their own experience, or knowledge they're gaining from their personal reading, or their work in other classes to imagine a more social or political kind of explanation for the gunman's behavior. "What might a sociologist say about this," we ask, "or your political science professor, or a member of the Women's Studies faculty?"

There are a number of directions the treatment of the analyzing strategy might take from here. Let us think of several immediate results from the work the class has done with this assignment, depending on the length of your term and the place of the assignment in your syllabus:

— No extended writing need be done; this assignment could be a warm-up for other analyzing assignments.

— Segments could lend themselves to 20- to 30-minute in-class writing. Having students summarize Seligman in their own words is a possibility, as is an exploratory comparison of the sort: "Briefly compare Seligman's theory with the explanation you developed for the gunman's behavior." (Either of these calls on previously mastered strategies.) Yet another possibility is for students to think through on paper their critique of Seligman's perspective.

— You could have the students attempt a rough draft of a paper using Seligman's theory to analyze the gunman's behavior. This could take anywhere from 45 minutes to two hours, and students wouldn't necessarily have to finish it. The paper would begin by posing the problem and summarizing Seligman, then applying Seligman's views to the hostage-taking.

— The assignment could be the basis for an extended, out-of-class paper. Such a paper might build from the rough draft mentioned previously, though it might also be developed without that rehearsal. This paper would require not only the application of Seligman's theory to the gunman's behavior but the incorporation — perhaps in a concluding paragraph — of a critique of the theory.

Options. To illustrate working with an option, we focus here on the History Option in the "Defining" chapter, which provides students a reading from Ted Howard and Jeremy Rifkin's book on the eugenics movement, *Who Should Play God?* We give students the following instructions:

> Some ideas can best be defined by describing the uses to which they have been put, their social history. In the following passage, notice how Ted Howard and Jeremy Rifkin, without offering a one-sentence definition, clarify the concept of *eugenics* by summarizing its history. Also notice that they offer this historical account from their own strong point of view as critics of those who favor genetic engineering. After reading their account several times, try sketching a summary of their summary. Then write an essay that defines eugenics from the historical point of view of Howard and Rifkin.

> As an alternative assignment, after reading Howard and Rifkin, write a speculative essay defining *genetic engineering*. As a phrase, what are its overtones? Why do you think that Howard and Rifkin are eager in their book to connect this term with *eugenics?* Does a dictionary give you any help with either term? Do you think that experimental scientists in the field of genetics use this term to define themselves and their work?

Once when we used this assignment, we introduced students to the defining strategy by having them do, at home, the problem on definitions of intelligence that opens the chapter and, in class, the assignment on word histories (First Pass #2). This was a fairly quick lead-in to an assignment as demanding as the Howard-Rifkin task, but, at that time, we were teaching in a ten-week quarter and wanted to get students working on rough drafts that could then be the subject of discussion and revision. If you have time, you might want to provide more preparation. But, still, none of the preceding assignments will fully prepare students to work with material that has the strong polemical edge of the excerpt on eugenics. That's one of the new challenges provided by the assignment.

The first drafts students produced from this assignment revealed interesting problems. A few drafts offered summaries of the Howard-Rifkin excerpt, but neglected to use the summary to construct a definition of *eugenics*. The papers followed the chronological order provided by Howard and Rifkin, but the history didn't emerge from or lead to definition. A few other drafts did provide a definition, but it was straight out of the dictionary, and the summary of eugenics history wasn't integrally connected to it. One paper begins thus:

> Ted Howard and Jeremy Rifkin describe how the word eugenics has been used in the past to determine how the present meaning has been developed. The present meaning of eugenics is defined as

> "the movement devoted to improving the human species through the control of heredity factors in mating."

The paper then goes on to summarize matter-of-factly the characters and events in the Howard-Rifkin excerpt. Here's an example:

> John Humphrey Noyes, founder of the Oneida Colony in N.Y. indirectly compared animals to the inferior race. "Every race horse, every straight-backed bull, every premium pig," said Noyes, "tells us what we can do and what we must do for man."

Such papers are pretty much a patchwork of assignment instructions, dictionary definitions, and textual quotations.

A third kind of draft attempted a definition that grew out of the history, but didn't adequately capture the critical perspective of the Howard-Rifkin discussion. One paper begins:

> As it is defined in most dictionaries, *eugenics* is "the science or study of heredity improvements." The definition implies that the human race can become even more superior . . . [and] this means breeding human beings to become more physically or mentally advanced. However, according to Ted Howard and Jeremy Rifkin, they imply a more definite or specific meaning of the word *eugenics*.

This writer goes on to summarize Howard and Rifkin selectively, and points out how definitions based on dictionary entries alone will lack precision, but does all this in a way that strips Howard and Rifkin of their argument.

Finally, there were drafts in which the authors attempted to develop a definition of *eugenics* out of the historical account and did so in a way that captured Howard and Rifkin's critical perspective. A few of these students even adopted that perspective:

> Eugenics is defined as a movement devoted to improving the human species by controlling heredity. This is the definition which is found in the dictionary, but Eugenics is much more than just controlling heredity. Eugenics is also the deliberate extermination of specific social classes and races . . . I believe that Ted Howard and Jeremy Rifkin would agree with me when I say that the dictionaries definition of eugenics doesn't come close to explaining what the full meaning of the word is.

The writer continues, selectively summarizing Howard and Rifkin, but in a way consonant with their argumentative thrust. For example:

> The recognized father of modern-day eugenics was Sir Francis Galton. Galton believed strongly in Charles Darwin's Theory of evolution and decided that he would try to apply this theory to human beings but by doing so Galton is responsible for giving people a "rationalization for the worst abuses of unrestrained capitalism and racism in America."

The range of critical acumen displayed in these drafts is likely to approximate the range you'll see in the papers your students will write early in the term.

In the following paragraphs we offer some thoughts on how to help students further develop their critical perspective.

Drafts like those just quoted will help you focus class discussion. The next class meeting we had after receiving these drafts, we posed the following questions:

— What do Howard and Rifkin seem to feel about the Eugenics movement? Is it appropriate to incorporate those feelings into a definition of a term like "eugenics"?

— How exactly does knowing the history of a word like *eugenics* help you define it? What did that history tell you?

— What feelings emerge in you as you read that history? How might those feelings shape your definition? Can a definition like this one be free of feeling and opinion? Should it be?

We had students revise after this discussion.

You can also use the drafts to organize writing groups. A good strategy is to place students so that each group represents a range of responses. We have been impressed with the way students pick up on the ambitious things their peers try and then attempt to improve their own drafts.

There are other ways to take advantage of the good work students produce in these first drafts. We try to establish right away an atmosphere in which students will feel comfortable learning from each other's work (assure them that this is *not* cheating). We talk about how professional writers rely on colleagues and editors, how often we ourselves must do that. Once students seem comfortable with us and each other, we often suggest in our written comments that one student might want to look at another's paper. Or we read sections from a particularly successful paper and ask the class to talk about what the writer is doing. Or when we're teaching more than one section of the same course, we'll select a few samples of a range of papers (with permission), remove the authors' names, photocopy and distribute them so that students are not working with papers from the same class they're in. (While positive examples can be used in the same class to good effect, negative examples usually create a stultifying discomfort — especially for the authors of those papers.) You can use these papers to spark discussion that leads to revision, have students play with rewriting the less developed papers, have them assess their own work in terms of the range of distributed papers, indicating the relative strengths and weaknesses of their own drafts.

And, of course, you can combine any of these approaches to suit your syllabus, class size, and time constraints.

Using Part Two

In this section, we would like to suggest some ways to work with Chapters 7–10. We'll concentrate on Chapter 9, "The Causes and Treatments of Schizophrenia," with the understanding that much of what we say is generally transferrable to "Women and Power," "Caribbean Fiction," and "Apes and Language."

Chapters 7–10 contain a hefty amount of material. They're meant to be individual sourcebooks of readings on complicated issues, providing more material than any one student could use in any one paper, but presenting at least some of the range and complexity of sources a student would encounter in a library search. "The Causes and Treatments of Schizophrenia" offers a rich mix of psychological, sociological, and biomedical perspectives, and it is one of the longer chapters in Part Two.

Note that we offer some advice on using particular readings and framing assignments further on in this instructor's manual, in the section on Chapter 9. We think new instructors, especially, might find this advice useful as they set out to work with this chapter. Our second piece of preliminary advice is this: It might be a good idea to skim the material in Chapter 9 before assigning it and then provide some guidance for students — pointing out readings that are more difficult, suggesting possible clusters and sequences of readings students interested in particular approaches to schizophrenia might take, and, when necessary, providing the orientation to difficult readings we mentioned earlier in this introduction. (Having a student's research materials before you enables you to provide more guidance and instruction on writing complex papers than would usually be possible.) This guidance inserts the teacher a bit more into the process of students' research than some might think ideal, but it does enable new teachers to have a better sense of what their students are about to take on and to better anticipate at least some of the problems their students might encounter. Before assigning a chapter like "The Causes and Treatments of Schizophrenia," you might want to consider the trade-offs between giving your students a free hand and providing them guidance. This tension is fundamental to the teaching of writing that is based on research and use of multiple sources. We hope that what follows will help you decide how to strike the balance that best suits your teaching style and pedagogical philosophy.

Many teachers have to work within time constraints that make it difficult to assign a chapter like "The Causes and Treatments of Schizophrenia" in its entirety. So we will demonstrate some ways we and colleagues of ours have tailored the chapter to squeeze it into the quarter or short semester.

One abbreviated assignment limits students to about 20 pages of reading. They read Shapiro, "History of the Concept of Schizophrenia" and "Description of and Diagnostic Criteria for Schizophrenia" and select one of the four case studies ("Diane Franklin," "John Fraser," "Ruby Eden," or "David G.") and argue that the person they selected is or is not schizophrenic according to the criteria presented in the first two readings. We have gotten some good papers in the two- to four-page range from this assignment.

You can make the assignment more complex by also requiring students to speculate about the cause or causes of the mental disturbance of the person they chose. Again, you can abbreviate and focus their reading by suggesting they look at Kohn, "The Interaction of Social Class and Other Factors in the Etiology of Schizophrenia"; Pato, Lander, and Schultz, "Prospects for the Genetic Analysis of Schizophrenia"; Thornton, "Family Issues in Schizophrenia"; Andreasen, "What Is Schizophrenia?"; and pp. 620–628 of Haley, "A Family Orientation." Adding this material brings the reading load to about 22 pages, still roughly half the length of the chapter. Some of these passages will probably need a brief orientation from you — and certainly small-group discussion would help a great deal — but they, as a whole, should not be beyond the general understanding of the average freshman class.

If these assignments are a little straightforward for your taste, and you'd rather assign one or more of the Options at the end of the chapter, but your experience with your class makes you worry that these questions might be tough going for them, providing some focus and selection with the readings might help. (We've found this approach helpful when assigning the chapter in so-called remedial classes.) Say, for example, a number of your students express an interest in Option #1:

> After reading the discussions of various kinds of therapies (drug therapy, psychotherapy, activities therapy) and the various modes of psychotherapy (individual, group, family, and family systems), draw up a treatment plan for one of the four cases on pp. 554–574. Be sure to justify your choices.

You might try focusing students' reading by having them review the four case studies and then turning to Thornton, "Family Issues in Schizophrenia," Bernheim and Lewine, "Treating the Schizophrenic Individual," Will, "Process, Psychotherapy, and Schizophrenia," Ciompi, "Consequences for Therapy," and Haley, "A Family Orientation." These readings alone (totaling approximately 32 pages) can result in effective papers, for students have to weigh competing assumptions about causality and claims about effectiveness.

The scope of this paper can be widened somewhat if students are asked also to read Mason, Gingerich, and Siris, "Patients' and Caregivers' Adaptation to Improvement in Schizophrenia" and Adler, "A Framework for the Analysis of Psychotherapeutic Approaches to Schizophrenia." These readings tend to complicate students' discussions of treatment plans and lead them to reconsider a fairly straightforward plan and/or redefine the issues represented by the case they've chosen.

There are a number of things you can do if you think your students need further assistance with any of the approaches we've suggested — and, of course, the big advantage in working with a self-contained selection of material is that you're able to provide such assistance in fairly specific ways.

— Preview readings or offer brief orientations to clusters of them — for example, the differences between individual therapy and group or activities therapies or the fundamental disagreement between Jay Haley and an individual-oriented therapist like Otto Will.

— Have students work in groups focused on topics they've chosen, readings they're analyzing, or writing assignments they're developing.

— Rely on journal writing or rough in-class papers to enable students to build facility and confidence with particular materials — for example, writing a personal reaction to a reading, or connecting it to events in one's own life or to the readings in other classes, or writing a one-paragraph summary of it.

— Ask individual students or groups to give brief progress reports on facts they're finding out and problems they're encountering, or give summaries of and reactions to particular issues or clusters of readings — for example, the previously mentioned contrast between Haley and Will.

The foregoing approaches to Chapter 9 place some constraints on students' engagement with materials and narrow the exploration and assessment of a wide range of sources that characterize research, but these approaches do make possible some work with multiple sources when time is short or when a teacher worries that the full range of materials on schizophrenia may be too difficult for his or her students to handle.

What if you *do* have adequate time with Chapter 9, and you do want your students to have the experience of sorting through a range of sources, but you are concerned that they may get lost in unproductive ways and you may lose touch with where they are? In that case, we offer one more suggestion as to how to structure students' engagement with "The Causes and Treatments of Schizophrenia." What we have done is provide a sequence of brief writing assignments that can lead to longer, more ambitious papers.

You can begin with a 15- or 20-minute freewrite on the topic "What is Madness?" Then have students read the material in the Framing the Issues section of the chapter: a poem, two pieces on defining and elaborating schizophrenia, and four case studies. After students do this reading, they can write one- or two-paragraph rough drafts responding to the questions in First Passes. These can be done in class or at home.

Students are then ready to choose material to read in the Complicating the Issues section — and you can provide as full or brief an orientation to the materials as you think they need. While they're exploring the materials — and depending on your time constraints, this might simply be a class period or a stretch of several days — they can do any of the following:

— Write brief, impressionistic responses to the readings that catch their attention — either in a positive or negative way

— Keep a running list of topics and issues that recur, or seem interesting, or need further clarification

— Explore the readings with their responses to the freewrite "What Is Madness?" and First Passes in hand, noting ways certain readings might enrich those earlier responses

— Explore the readings with the list of Options in hand, to see whether any of the questions emerge as interesting or do-able or helpful in focusing their reading

They will then be ready to begin their major paper on Chapter 9. And at this stage you can create further brief writing assignments that will help them develop their arguments. Let us imagine that the students in your class have chosen to work on the following Options:

2. In reading the various authors on schizophrenia, you'll notice that some tend to talk about schizophrenia as a medical-biological illness while others tend to talk in different ways: in terms of defects in adjustment or complications of family organization, for example. In your opinion, what are the advantages and disadvantages of these different perspectives? After presenting these, argue for the legitimacy of one over the others, or argue for an integration of all of them. Use material from cases and discussions of research and theory to support your position.

5. Using both the discussions by psychologists and psychiatrists and material from the accounts of schizophrenic patients, write a paper arguing that schizophrenia is primarily a devastation of the ability to form close relationships.

7. Using material from cases as well as from theoretical discussions, argue that when they're acting "crazy," schizophrenic

individuals are exhibiting understandable human concerns and, to the best of their ability at the moment, responding to those concerns.

9. Argue that families have been unfairly blamed for causing schizophrenia. Begin your paper with a summary of the various ways families have been suggested as the source of schizophrenic illness, then you can go on to argue for the inadequacies of or problems with these perspectives.

11. After reading Mason, Gingerich, and Siris's article "Patients' and Caregivers" Adaptation to Improvement in Schizophrenia," create an imaginary dialogue in which therapists and patients — select at least three — respond to the authors' observations and suggestions. What would any of the people in the four case studies or the person in "Can We Talk?" have to say? How about Jay Haley or Luc Ciompi or John Thornton, or any of the others? What do you think they would have to say?

We've found that even a range of questions usually provides opportunity for a general assignment that students can apply to their own work. The preceding list, for example, gives rise to issues of definition and to a number of potentially valuable comparisons. You could ask students to begin their project by writing brief, and not necessarily polished, papers defining "medical-biological" or "family organization" or "crazy" or "relationship" and/or papers comparing terms ("biological" and "environmental") or readings (the opening poem and "Can We Talk?" or the pieces by Luc Ciompi and Jay Haley). These papers can be discussed in small groups or can be quickly and generally assessed by you during workshop. Or, time permitting, you can use them to provide suggestions as to what students need to spend more time on or work on next, or further issues they might consider.

We sometimes forget — for we developed our own skill at it some time ago — how hard it is to learn how to conduct effective library research and to write from multiple sources. Chapters 7–10 remove some of the uncertainty from the process and establish some constraints so that students will be able to take on such work within the limits of the freshman composition class and so that their teachers — working with a bounded set of materials shared by the class — can guide and assist in their growth. In doing such work, the teacher must decide many times along the way when to intercede and when to let students be. We hope we've been able to provide some approaches and techniques for those times when you think it will be helpful to give some direction to students who are working with a range of complex materials and difficult questions.

Suggestions on the Research Chapters, 11 and 12. In the research chapters, Framing the Issues comprises not readings but guidelines and directions for conducting field research. More so than for Chapters 7–10, students can produce full, complex papers by working with the selections in Framing the Issues alone. (Though the directions in the First Passes suggest that students write brief responses to the questions there, they could easily produce much longer essays from the data they collect in their field research.) But if you or your students desire, the data they collect in Framing the Issues can also be analyzed with the help of brief readings contained in Complicating the Issues. Options, which follow Complicating the Issues, offer a range of questions that require some integration of field research and the readings.

We probably don't need to say much about the directions for gathering field data: They're fairly explicit and uncomplicated. It's important to urge students, though, to begin collecting their data as soon as possible after a research chapter has been assigned or selected. You might build in some means to check on their progress — and it can be informal. Have students write a brief summary of the material they're collecting or, if it can be displayed, have them show you or the class some of what they're finding: cartoons, journal articles, and so on. Since many of your students will not have conducted this kind of research before, some might underestimate what's required or might run into methodological problems: How do I take notes when someone's telling a joke? How do I try to distinguish among the kinds of speech I hear in a lecture, a quiz section, and a tutoring session? There might even be technical problems: where to place the tape recorder, how to make oneself unobtrusive. All such questions and problems can create the occasion for informative class or small group discussions and/ or for brief, informal papers on method. Since issues of methodology go right to the heart of academic work, these discussions and papers can turn problems into rich opportunities for learning about academic research firsthand. You might even raise fundamental questions like: How do you think your presence (at a tutoring session, during the telling of a joke) affected what was said, the data you collected?

If you do move on to the readings in Complicating the Issues, you might try some of the suggestions we offer in our discussion of Chapter 9: previewing readings; indicating common themes; having students write brief impressions of the readings, discuss them in groups, and so on.

Perhaps the most helpful thing we can suggest about the two research chapters is to have fun with them. Yes, you will need to provide some guidance and monitor student progress and create opportunities for students to talk through the problems they're encountering. But, in our experience, students who research the comic have a good time and are continually bringing to class funny stories and flashes of insight about what's funny and why. And those who research the discourse of their major begin to understand some important things about higher education and feel a bit less mystified by it all. It is not uncommon — and this can be a powerful byproduct of working with Chapter 12 — for students to reconsider the major they've chosen as they pursue their research. In fact, one thing you could ask students to do is to reflect on their choice of major in the context of the research they're conducting. This can lead to some invigorating class discussion that, in various ways, plays off and feeds into the writing they've been doing all term.

Working with Your Students

Stimulating Classroom Discussion

We think that *Critical Strategies* can be taught most effectively if you organize your classroom as a workshop where the focus is on student writing — doing it, talking about it, responding to it — and the teacher's role is primarily that of a facilitator. Running a writing class as a workshop will provide a tremendous relief from many of the worries that vex new teachers, though it will require you to bring to bear a range of organizational and interpersonal skills.

The workshop format has many benefits. You don't have to have a full hour or two of material prepared, you're not always "on," your expertise is not always on the line. A good deal of the writing that gets done won't require your formal evaluation. Responsibility is shared; in some ways, the students are carrying more of the instructional burden than you are. What the workshop format does require from the instructor is the thoughtful planning of the general structure of a given class: topics, assignments, and materials. It requires the ability to pose thought-provoking questions and the willingness to listen carefully to the ensuing discussion, moving in and out of it to clarify a student's comment, or to connect a comment to an earlier one, or to help the group focus a discussion or redirect it in a promising direction. It calls for a willingness to assist in the development of a thought and an equal willingness to step back, to create room for students to think things through. At the heart of it, such a class calls for a balance between providing direction and honoring spontaneity and a belief in students' ability to do rigorous and interesting intellectual work.

Let us make this more concrete by presenting several excerpts from a recent class. This class was working with the Option in the "Comparing" chapter that presents two accounts of creation, one from an indigenous Australian tribe, the other from current Big Bang theory.

The teacher began with a brief general discussion of the strategy of comparing, noting that students are most likely familiar with the strategy and asking for a few examples from their school experience. The students cited examples from exams, and one or two mentioned longer papers they had to do in high school — for example, comparing two characters from Shakespeare. After about five or ten minutes — enough to establish the common utility of the comparing strategy and to call up students' own experience with it — the teacher turned to the assignment and asked for volunteers to summarize the Australian account.

Then the students took over. Tracy started by saying that she couldn't pronounce some of the words (and the teacher agreed that he couldn't either), but then went on to do a good job of recounting the myth. The teacher complimented her and asked if anyone had anything else to add. Carmen noted a few things Tracy omitted and pointed out what she saw as a contradiction: "If this is a story about the beginning of everything, then why are there already men alive? . . . It says here that 'men saw a new light appearing.' That doesn't make sense to me." The teacher admitted that that seemed puzzling and opened Carmen's problem to class discussion. Discussion picked up for a few minutes, but didn't resolve the problem Carmen posed, so the teacher, checking his watch, noted that they should move onto "Big Bang," but said that they would return to this problem.

Before moving to our second excerpt, let's dwell for a moment on what this teacher was doing.

— The teacher set the stage, provided context, associated current work with student experience.

— The teacher shifted the focus to the students, encouraging further discussion and posing problems drawn from student commentary.

— Though the students carried the discussion, the teacher listened closely, respectfully, and facilitated while keeping an eye on the time.

The class then turned to the account of the Big Bang, and Sam immediately said that though he got the general idea, he found some of the sentences hard to understand because he never had studied astronomy. "That's OK, that happens all the time," said the teacher. "In college, you're going to be reading stuff you don't fully understand." He then pointed out to Sam that though Sam had some trouble with specific sentences, he kept on reading and was able to get the general idea. "This is a valuable strategy," he observed, "for gaining a general understanding of readings that, at first, seem too specialized or difficult." Then the teacher asked the physical science majors in the class to explain some of the more technical material. What they offered helped — and there was further discussion. He asked if anyone else had difficulty with the reading, or had reservations, or questions. No one said they did. So members of the class proceeded to summarize the account of the Big Bang.

The teacher broke the class into small groups of two and three students, asking them to "sketch or list some differences and some similarities between these two accounts of creation." He noted that several differences probably came to mind right away, but that "it might be especially interesting to think hard about possible similarities." The teacher tried to form the groups in ways that would enhance interaction; speculating that Robert and Minnie and Hiep might produce interesting results because their majors ranged from dance to computer science; remembering that the last time he put Sarah with Betsy, Sarah dominated the conversation and so this time pairing them differently.

The groups worked for about 15 minutes, then their energy began to wane: The teacher overheard one group talking about last night's basketball game, noticed the members of another beginning to break up on their own. So he called the class back to gather the fruits of their work.

Before moving to the final excerpt, let's again reflect on what this teacher did. The teacher

— Encouraged students to voice the difficulties or reservations they might be having with a reading or an assignment, and turned these into topics of class discussion
— Called attention to effective reading and writing strategies individual students were using, and called the other students' attention to these strategies
— Drew on the collective knowledge in the classroom to assist in clarifying assignments and materials
— Created opportunities for the students to work together. (He tried to group students in productive ways, provided some direction, and called the class back together when the groups seemed to be winding down.)

Next, the teacher went to the board and began listing, in two columns, the similarities and differences the students found. Sarah said one difference was that the Big Bang passage is scientific and the other passage is make-believe, a story. The teacher listed "science vs. make-believe" on the board and asked Sarah if there was another word she could use for "make-believe"; she looked quickly at the textbook and said "myth." "OK," the teacher said and substituted "myth" for "make-believe," asking her as he did so if she could provide any evidence from the text to support this difference. "Look right at the language, Sarah. What's the difference even in the language?" Sarah studied the texts for a moment and responded: "Well, the 'Big Bang' uses all kinds of scientific words and numbers, but the myth uses . . . like . . . well, 'in the beginning,' and people's names, and descriptions of plants and places, and all that." The teacher put this linguistic distinction on the board, asking the class, as he did so, for examples from "the Big Bang theory" of "words that let us know we're in the realm of science" — and the class offered examples: "protons, neutrons, electrons," "10^8K," "isotope," and so on.

This activity continued a while longer — with the class listing new similarities and differences — then one of the students, Chip, observed that "Maybe that first difference about science vs. myth isn't really a difference. I mean," he continued, "it's not like they actually saw the Big Bang." The teacher encouraged Chip to continue. Chip said he couldn't say what he meant, and the teacher pointed out that he just said something interesting about the astronomy passage and asked him what triggered that observation in the first place. "Go back and look at the passage, Chip; see if you can recall what made you come up with this observation."

Further discussion ensued, then the teacher, checking some brief notes he scribbled earlier, returned to the issue that Carmen posed. "It might be good now to raise an issue Carmen brought up a while back. She said that if this myth is supposed to be depicting creation, then why are there already people alive in this story?" He asked Carmen to elaborate, and she did. Then he said: "Think about the way each of these accounts presents events, how each is structured, the logic of each. Let's begin with "the Big Bang theory". Can someone trace the order of the events, what comes first, second, third? . . ."

Discussion continued; then the teacher posed a writing assignment that would take up the remainder of this two-hour class. He asked the students to pick one similarity and one difference that most interested them and write a brief, rough comparison. He asked them for thoughts on how such a comparison might be structured, put some of this on the board, and added suggestions of his own. The students began writing, and the teacher circulated around the room, sometimes sitting with a student for a few minutes to discuss a problem, sometimes asking to read what a student was producing, sometimes getting two students together who might benefit from seeing what each other was doing.

Let's reflect on what the teacher did. The teacher

— Acted as scribe to the students' ideas, but asked questions to clarify or expand the discussion
— Provided assistance to help students articulate and support their observations
— Connected the discussion to other important material when possible, both from the text and from student discussion.
— Created opportunities for students to practice writing, to rehearse with a good deal of feedback but little formal evaluation

We hope these excerpts give you a sense of how to organize a class as a writing workshop. We must point out, though, that what we presented illustrates one of the many ways a workshop can be organized. Other emphases and structures are possible. Our notion of workshop involves a fair degree of orchestration and what some educators working in the tradition of Russian psychologist Lev Vygotsky call "assisted performance." There are other ways to run a workshop. Some creative writing workshops, for example, are conducted more by the students themselves, and some composition classes are organized around student-initiated projects taking their direction from emerging student work.

We prefer the model we illustrated because, in our experience, students are not very familiar with the things *Critical Strategies* asks them to do, and they welcome some assistance, some orchestration of classroom activity, and some clock-watching. If this rationale sounds right to you, but your bent is toward more student-initiated projects or more collaborative learning, then, of course, you could begin the quarter or semester in the manner illustrated above but move toward student-initiated projects. One teacher we know used Part Two of the book in this way, having students choose the chapter that most interested them, work together to arrive at paper topics, and report on their evolving projects to the class.

Responding to Student Writing

Some of the writing a curriculum like ours encourages will seem to violate many of the standards of good expository prose, though, we hope, the end result will be students' willingness to enter into complicated discursive territory, exhibit a degree of comfort and sophistication with academic writing, and produce a thoughtful and reflective prose. We believe, however, that if we want to see a pleasing final product, then we need to create space in our classrooms where students can write messily, inelegantly, awkwardly. For students to achieve any level of sophistication with critical writing, they'll need to be encouraged to rehearse, to approximate, to have multiple opportunities to try out an idea or a strategy or a syntactic move. That means they must take chances to stretch beyond what they can safely do.

And the resulting prose might be ungrammatical and inelegant. In fact, *not* to point out error, not to correct and model masterful prose might well seem a dereliction of duty. But at times you'll need to hold off, to look instead for a germinating idea, or an approximation of a rhetorical strategy — and encourage the student to move on. For it is often through a series of approximations — tentative, not perfect — that we develop competence. Let us illustrate.

Many times during class, we'll ask students to write for five or ten minutes: to offer an opinion about a reading or discussion, to express in their own words a critical insight arrived at in class, to construct a brief summary of a reading, and so on. Obviously, these bits of writing will be tentative, unrevised, flawed. The purpose of this work is not to correct grammar and syntax, or to work toward more graceful sentence structure or diction, but to listen for insight, to get a sense of whether the student is catching on to the way a strategy works, to note if the student is proceeding logically, using evidence to support his or her points, and so on.

The following example comes from the opening problem in the "Classifying" chapter on metaphors about writing. We asked students to read a series of metaphors about the composing process taken from interviews with professional writers and "develop a classification scheme to identify the different ways these writers talk about the act of writing." This excerpt is the beginning of a student's response to the assignment:

> Authors use a variety of metaphors to describe their writing processes. These metaphors can be discussed in many ways such as: Arts, medium, mechanical, and organic things. Sometimes a writer will describe their writing by way of sculpting or painting. William Goyen and Laura Chester express their writing in terms of molding, sculpting, chiseling and sculpture, whereas Albert Moravia and Gore Vidal describe it as painters doing a painting. . . .

There are grammatical problems to be addressed in the excerpt as well as some problems with phrasing — and the teacher will want to get to them if they remain in later drafts — but we think the most fruitful move to make with this early draft would be to ask the student if sculpting and painting convey similar or different things to her, what images come to mind when she imagines each, what processes she imagines a sculptor or a painter using. Questions like these help the student think about the classification scheme she's devising and can lead to a second set of questions: Why would a writer compare his or her writing to sculpting or painting? What about these acts might be similar, what is the writer trying to convey about writing that the use of metaphor helps achieve? Finally, you might point out how helpful it would be for readers to have some of these metaphors in front of them, for the student to work Goyen's and Chester's and Moravia's and Vidal's metaphors into the discussion.

And there will be times when it might be inadvisable to worry about correctness at all. Consider this response to the invitation to create a metaphor that best describes the student's own composing processes:

> For me, writing is very much like a thunderstorm. All my ideas
> comes flashing through my head and pouring down on my paper.
> and I'd write it down violently, then after a few minutes it starts
> to calm down and then I collect the scribble of ideas that was
> scattered on my paper.

This was written by the same young woman whose work we present above, and what's interesting here, it seems to us, is the originality of her metaphor: It is unlike those of the professional writers in the assignment she was working on. We're struck, too, by the internal consistency of the metaphor (though the end needs some work) and, in fact, by the degree to which it seems to represent her composing process, as we've observed her writing in class. One possible next move would be to encourage her to play out the last stage of her metaphor, the calm after the thunderstorm and the "collecting of the scribbles." Then we'd pose questions to get her to think about placing her metaphor in the category system she created for the metaphors of the professional writers. What does she make of the fact that it doesn't really fit? We'd also ask her to consider the difference in the styles of her two pieces of writing, both produced quickly in class, and ask her to think about ways she might get some of the flair of the latter into the former. At this point, we might ask her to experiment, to take that earlier piece of writing and recast it. Finally we might encourage her to develop her metaphor into a final section for her paper classifying the professional writers, one that situates her metaphor in relation to the professionals and discusses what it reveals about her composing process. And then, of course, we could begin to shift focus to issues of correctness.

A general principle for using *Critical Strategies* would be this: There can be pedagogical value in momentarily suspending concerns about correctness and stylistic grace. This principle, as we've tried to show, can apply to thought pieces, rehearsals, and early drafts, but it can apply over longer series of assignments as well. Working with *Critical Strategies* does not lead to the production of isolated products, assignments that have no connection to each other — rather, the pedagogical effects are cumulative. Therefore, it is possible that your focus on issues of correctness and style would increase over the term, as students develop skill with the strategies and become more critical in their perspective.

A Note on Classroom Atmosphere

In our experience, the curriculum advocated in *Critical Strategies* works best in a certain kind of classroom. The structure we prefer, as we've noted, is that of a workshop, but there's still the issue of the mood or tone of the room, its ethos or atmosphere, regardless of how the class is organized. Trying to give written advice about creating a particular classroom atmosphere is about as difficult as giving advice in writing about saying the comforting thing in a delicate romance or singing a song with just the right lilt, but the issue is such an important one that we'd feel this introduction would be incomplete without it.

We've found that *Critical Strategies* works best in a classroom in which there are high expectations and an abiding belief in students' abilities to engage in rigorous intellectual work, but in which students feel free to think out loud, to see where a line of thought will lead them, to make mistakes, to say the obvious, to blunder and be inarticulate, and to work toward a critical position via pop cultural references and slang and sentiment. To create such a place, the teacher of English will often need to suspend early judgment and ask the encouraging question instead; to suppress the witty jab, the clever retort; to accept the obvious as a legitimate place to start. And the atmosphere that results will produce some remarkable moments. Here are several examples.

This class had been working on the Option in the "Comparing" chapter that presents two accounts of creation. The teacher had introduced the assignment and the class was in the process of summarizing the two different accounts — one a myth, the other from Western astronomy — when Tony blurted out about the myth: "Hey, I see: Is this their way of explaining how creation came about?" The teacher came close to asking Tony where he'd been for the last 15 minutes — "Earth to Tony," or some such jab — when he checked the impulse and asked instead what led Tony to say that. Tony pointed to the opening, "In the very beginning . . ." The teacher turned to the class and asked "What are the first words in the Bible?" The class responded.

"Does anyone know of other creation myths?" the teacher then asked, and several students offered answers. Then the teacher posed the question: "Why do you suppose people create these myths?" And William, who was born in Saigon in 1972, said: "You want to know where you come from. This might seem off the track a little, but you take me. I was in an orphanage for three years before my parents adopted me. And a lot of times I wonder about my original parents, what they were like, and all, and I make up stories about them. These myths are like that — people trying to imagine how they got here."

One more. The class was discussing the Gary Soto poem "Oranges" (part of an assignment in the "Comparing" chapter). In the poem, a boy out on his first date finds that he doesn't have enough money to buy his girlfriend a candy bar. He has five cents and two oranges in his pockets, and in desperation hands the saleslady his nickel and one of his oranges. The saleslady's eyes meet his, "knowing/Very well what it was all/About," and accepts the nickel and the orange. Later:

I took my girl's hand
In mine for two blocks,
Then released it to let
Her unwrap the chocolate.
I peeled my orange

That was so bright against
The gray of December
That, from some distance,
Someone might have thought
I was making a fire in my hands.

When the teacher asked the class what was going on here, Abby said, "They're buying an orange." Several students immediately disagreed, and Inez turned to her and without judgment, said, "He had the oranges, and he used one to pay for the candy bar." Abby lit up, "Oh, I get it, jeez." She seemed not embarrassed at her misreading but pleased to see the events making a new kind of sense to her. The teacher asked her if this new understanding contributed anything to her reading of the poem. She looked back at the text, looked up and said: "Yeah. At the end now where he's peeling the orange — it's like there's a certain spark. Like making fire."

It is interesting to think about the conditions that can foster such rich associations and flashes of insight. Certainly, the classroom has to be a place where intellectual work is valued. But just as important, we've come to believe, is the need for the classroom to be a safe place — a place where students are encouraged to say what comes to mind, and push harder, and haltingly follow a thought.

William's association to his origins and Abby's insight about "Oranges" emerged, we're convinced, because there was a certain kind of social-intellectual freedom in their class. We wonder what might have happened if, as a matter of course, the teacher had taken his jab at Tony for his delayed awareness or in some way embarrassed Abby for her misreading. We can't say for sure, of course, but, in our experience, the kind of class that would be characterized by such response limits the possibilities for students to display their intelligence.

To advocate this kind of freedom is *not* to say a teacher should let mistakes or lack of effort go unchecked. That would be patronizing. Rather, the challenge is to create a place where serious but adventurous intellectual work can get done, a place that is simultaneously rigorous and nurturing.

Part One

Critical Strategies

Chapter 1

Defining (p. 10)

We offer these remarks by Neil Postman in the spirit of this chapter:

> Most people are overcome by a sort of intellectual paralysis when
> confronted by a definition, whether offered by a politician or by a
> teacher. They fail to grasp that a definition is not a manifestation
> of nature but merely and always an instrument for helping us to
> achieve our purposes. . . . It is essential that [students] understand
> that definitions are hypotheses and that embedded in each is a
> particular philosophical or political or epistemological point of
> view. It is certainly true that he who holds the power to define is
> our master, but it is also true that he who holds in mind an
> alternative definition can never quite be his slave. (*Conscientious
> Objections*, 1988)

Or she either.

Working with the Strategy

The introductory section for each chapter is intended to be as interactive as
possible, something that's hard to convey in print. Since many students tend
to read fairly passively, waiting for answers — or at least for someone else to
formulate the questions — you might want to preview some of the readings and
exercises we walk through in the text.

At the start, for example, you might ask students to attempt a written
definition of intelligence and then to talk both about the content of their definitions and about the process of defining a word. They could then consider how
their definitions do and do not fit within the categories proposed in the introduction to Ulrich Neisser's essay (p. 10). Certainly the writing they do, both before
and after reading Neisser's essay, can be rough. Journals might be a good place
for much of this exploratory writing, especially since you may want to return
to earlier readings later in the course.

As students work with Neisser's essay, they are, in some ways, previewing the rest of their work with this textbook. The author uses both classification and comparison in the process of defining intelligence; students can discuss both the categories he creates and the strength of the comparison. Do they, for example, see other kinds of "intelligence" that these two categories do not include? This kind of thinking encourages them to question classification systems, asking both how they help us to see and how they limit our vision. And is the comparison with courage convincing? Again, in what ways does it expand our understanding of intelligence, and in what ways is it limiting? Are students inclined to see intelligence as more monolithic than courage? If so, why? And what examples can they provide to support their observations?

After considering Neisser's essay, students are asked to pause to think about their thinking process (p. 13). This might be a good time to discuss their notions of definition. As we know, many students have heard repeated directions to "look it up in the dictionary" to find "the correct definition." In this chapter, the primary emphasis is on complicating this overly simplistic approach and on suggesting that the negative connotations that surround it might be replaced by a more dynamic and interesting notion of what definition is, where it comes from, and how it works. The questions about thinking and the remainder of the introductory material ask for consideration of these issues.

Cases

The readings and explanations in this section should provide interesting material for class discussion interspersed with frequent short writing tasks. Asking students to first write something brief about the word *model, refugee,* or *hysteria* may help them read the material more aggressively and thoughtfully, with some sense of preliminary investment.

The Case of *model* (p. 15)

In fact, to prepare for the discussion of how a curious reader might gradually define the word *model,* you might help students develop a preliminary exercise. Ask for both a definition and a specific example; then try pooling both to try out the definitions. Do any of them fit most of the examples? Do some fit better than others? Why? Are there some that fit all the examples but too loosely to be of any real help to our understanding?

On page 17, you might ask students why we have used an example from a dictionary published in 1975. The practical answer is that more recent editions are more cognizant of the meaning of the term *model* now in vogue in academic writing. It's a graphic example of how meanings can shift in emphasis over time.

Cases from Political Science (p. 18)

Work with the word *refugee* might include a side excursion to a recent newspaper article about refugees and a discussion of how the definitions offered apply to the current situation. Similarly, if you choose to engage students in discussion of the coup d'état/surgery/takeover analogy, recent accounts of all three might prove helpful. Most students do not know enough about coups d'état or takeovers to be able to develop the analogy without some assistance. Nevertheless, with or without a bit of research, group discussion to develop the analogy might be fun as students see both the power and the limits of analogy.

A Case from Psychology (p. 21)

Our colleague Ellen Quandahl used the complete *Dora* (it's a short book) as the basis of several writing assignments in classes she taught in the Freshman Preparatory Program at UCLA. (She has written about the experience in "Freud and the Teaching of Interpretation" by Patricia Donahue and Ellen Quandahl, *College English* 49:6 [October 1987]:641–49). Students find the book tough going at first, but it also reads enough like a detective story that students get hooked firmly to the narrative — despite Freud's piecemeal way of constructing it. And once hooked, they are ready to think analytically about Freud's language and method of analysis. Freud offers rich illustration of what Postman maintains in the quotation that opened this chapter: Definitions are hypotheses. Many students develop a perceptively ambivalent attitude toward Freud, an attitude which may serve them well later. And they leave the course with the sense that they've taken on a difficult and academically representative book. If you're ever looking for a book to fulfill those functions . . .

First Passes

Several of the relatively brief readings in this section can provide material for reading, discussion, and writing done entirely in class. At-home assignments might include further work with word histories and consideration of the longer piece by Nancy Mairs, at the end of the section.

1. Defining from Context (p. 25)

We think students need to become aware of this general intellectual problem: It's often easier to deal with the strange terms we know we don't know than the familiar ones we think we do. The examples we offer here are arbitrary, of course, and we can't claim to have solved the problem of how to keep students alert to this pitfall as they read. It might be interesting to see whether students who are asked to keep a reader's journal over the course of the term will begin to regloss such terms on their own.

Qualified. Most students will write "having an ability," "suitable," "competent," "fit to perform the job." What's revealing about the reading passage is that when this meaning of *qualified* is imported to it, the passage is not made much more incomprehensible (which would be a tip-off that something is wrong) but only blurred. The sentence in which the word occurs is already so abstract (the double negative doesn't help either) that misreading *qualified* is not likely to be the major problem in reading the passage. To see the problem, we need first to decode the jargon.

> If this point of view is not to be absurdly naive, it must be qualified by the realization that it is not universally valid by any means.

Defogged, this becomes:

But this point of view is naive, unless qualified.

And now we can ask, "What does *qualified* seem to mean?"

If you find working with this paragraph worth the labor it takes, you might want to consider this little spin-off definition assignment: Write two definitions of the term *civilized*, one with which the author would agree and one with which he would not.

Accommodations. Misread, this sentence seems to be saying something about living conditions, a reading that is oddly supported by the phrasing "congealed into large units" and, two sentences later, the word *household*. Students have taken the general meaning to be that president Lyndon Johnson felt cramped in the city and hankered for open Texas spaces. But if students can sustain this misreading for most of the paragraph, they should nevertheless be puzzled by the reappearance of *accommodation* in the last sentence. Why must we decide that the word refers to a state of mind?

Mechanism. The passage from Stephen Jay Gould makes two uses of the term. Both uses depart from our contemporary sense of something mechanical. But it may be worth distinguishing between Gould's two uses of the term. The second usage, *mechanisms* as "contrivances" to ensure pollination, seems quite close to the *machine* meaning, a sort of figurative extension from machines to flowers. But the first use of the term is much more abstract: natural selection as the "primary mechanism" of evolution. It's hard — at least it should be hard, shouldn't it? — to see the machine here. Or to see the process of evolution as a machine is to challenge our usual definition of *machine*. *Mechanism*, we probably decide, needs to be taken away from the machines.

The suggestions and questions to consider should provide students with sufficient direction to begin definitions; you might want to recommend that they return to the model used for *model* or *refugee* to work out definitions for these terms.

2. Word Histories (p. 26)

The idea for this assignment was furnished by our colleague Mike Gustin.

Our reasons for choosing these particular words were not elaborate. We chose words that had specific points of origin, or interesting shifts of meaning, or strange bifurcations, or gradual but palpable alterations over time. Instead of working with our selections, you might want to send your class off to the library on individualized research missions of their own (or your) choosing.

The abbreviation system of the *Oxford English Dictionary* is a bit daunting, but students seem to enjoy demystifying it a bit. It's worth asking students to look in some detail at the sample entry on career. Get them to notice how selectively the entry has been treated.

To expand this assignment after working through one or more of the given examples as a class, you might want to send students (individually or as small groups) to find, write a short essay about, and bring to class to share, words of their own choosing. Selecting the details that will enable them to present a brief history of a word that interests them is a helpful exercise not only in definition but also in selection and organization.

In addition, students may be interested to look at the monthly feature "Word Watch" in the *Atlantic*, a page presenting words that are entering the language and being tracked for possible dictionary inclusion. This practice neatly dispels the myth that words and their definitions are fixed and unchanging.

3. Redefining (p. 30)

As students approach the piece by Nancy Mairs, they may find it helpful first to consider their own responses to the words *handicap* and *cripple* and to begin to think about the ways words color both how and what we see.

The question of who defines is also significant here; as students consider times when others have defined them differently from the way(s) they have defined themselves, they may begin to see that definition involves ownership of language as well as tapping into shared meaning — and that definition often involves emotion as well as what they may regard as static meaning.

Mairs's essay is likely to evoke a strong emotional response that can be used to focus discussion on the issues of definition: Who does the defining? What are the emotional connotations of words? What expectations do words conjure in listeners and readers? How do our definitions of *woman* and *doctor* play into Mairs's experience?

If the discussion is lively and you want to expand on this assignment, you could take a look at "Defiantly Incorrect" by Timothy Egan, an article about cartoonist John Callahan (*New York Times Magazine, June 7, 1992*). Callahan's cartoons portray people with all kinds of handicaps (the artist himself is quadriplegic) with an irreverence that has angered some and delighted others. Students should find the article an interesting companion piece for Mairs's essay, either now or in connection with the analysis chapter, when they are looking at one text in light of another.

Options

In this section, students will find writings about definition from several academic fields. One useful way to proceed through this material is to allow students, working individually or as groups, to choose selections that interest them or relate to their major fields. They could work their responses into short essays, into longer pieces if you prefer, or into brief presentations to make during a class period. You'll want to include a time at the end for summary and for reflection — either oral or in journal entries — to explore what working with these selections contributes to understanding of both the process of definition and the particular issues discussed in the selections.

This assignment complements the discussion of the term *model*, pages 15–18.

A Biology Option (p. 39)

Hypertension might be defined as "high blood pressure," a definition that seems little more than tautology. To convert this static definition into something more explanatory means seeing hypertension as something ongoing, not a thing but an event. What this exercise asks of students is one example of what Young, Becker, and Pike (in *Rhetoric, Discovery, and Change*) mean by "tagmemic analysis." As a heuristic device, they recommend looking at an object of inquiry alternatively as "particle, wave, and field." We gain definition by looking at something in itself (as a particle), as a process (wave), and as a context for looking at other sub-events (as a field). Biological terms are always good candidates for these kinds of conversions, for most biological terms need to be understood by plugging them into some larger picture and they also lend themselves to being opened up to more detailed investigation. This is also a good general technique in dealing with definitions in history classes — the Missouri compromise, for example, can be seen as particle, wave, or field.

A Genetics Option (p. 40)

Repeating a strategy used at the start of the chapter, students might begin by defining sexual reproduction as they understand it. Ask any biology majors in the class to explain their understanding of the term in the scientific context. Exploring their own ideas on the subject may help students to grasp the complexity of Jacquard's argument. To read this selection passively may well be to miss the point.

As students work with the selection, it will be important to point to the issues that complicate the central question, to the way Jacquard attacks the "but of course" approach to the subject in favor of a more complex view. They will, of course (!), notice the use of *model* (p. 15) and connect it to their earlier discussion. The historical growth and change of the definition and of the understanding of the process is also important, as is true for more scientific knowledge. Students can examine the way each theory expands, explains, and refines the concept. In fact, if scientists in the class are willing to share their knowledge, it might be fun for them to present other examples of knowledge and understanding that have shifted and, therefore, altered definitions, over time. Equally interesting is an exploration of the social context of definition: Word meanings are rarely developed outside a particular social context, and shifts in meaning often connect to larger social shifts.

A History Option (p. 45)

Although we're concerned with defining, we're also introducing summarizing: Working with these passages calls for searching out meaningful generalizations and presenting those generalizations in a coherent way. The intent is not merely to underscore the perception that words *have* histories but that histories must be given shape.

Dictionaries are apt to define *eugenics* as "the study of hereditary improvements." One way to give this assignment a strong argumentative slant is to ask students why Howard and Rifkin would not accept this definition.

A fundamental question: Why does the term *eugenics* have such a strong negative connotation? Ask students whether they think this is only Howard and Rifkin's point of view, or whether the word usually carries taint.

Ted Howard and Jeremy Rifkin's book is a diatribe against genetic engineering (Rifkin is well known as the most persistent gadfly of the biological establishment), and it's interesting to see that part of their technique is to make genetic engineering guilty by association. By placing recent genetic work in the tradition of *eugenics*, they make that work suspect by association. But there's no reason to assume that the shoddy science of the one has been passed along to the other.

Before asking students to write about eugenics, you might ask them to work with a few preliminary assignments of the sort we've presented as First Passes above. One spin-off is to ask students to write a short paragraph differentiating *eugenics* and *genetics*. Another might be to try, whether working from this article, or from their general knowledge, or from some other particular source, to differentiate *eugenics* and *genetic engineering*.

The term *genetic engineering* (which does not appear in our excerpt) is a good example of a term whose definition is politicized. If you ask students to speak or write about it, you might want to call attention to how much of the debate about the idea is already structured by the phrase itself: What are the connotations, positive and negative, of the term *engineering*, and what are the overtones of yoking it to a biological word?

The reading itself is not so much an effort to define eugenics historically as to dramatize the snowballing of an idea under the mantle of scientific respectability. There's a kind of revisionist history of American icons tainted by gullibility: Calvin Coolidge, Margaret Sanger, Alexander Graham Bell, the Boy Scouts . . . Howard and Rifkin seem to encourage reading this list with smug superiority. But there's another way of reading this that may be closer to the authors' intents: how susceptible are we still to scientific authority? How little warrant will suffice for a culture to accept as *scientific* something they are predisposed to believe?

A Philosophy Option (p. 51)

This passage by Peter Singer won't support a lengthy piece of writing, but it calls for some sharp reading and thinking. We see this work with clearly differentiated perspectives as anticipatory of the Analyzing chapter.

Students may have trouble finding in the piece the three perspectives we ask about, since the first, the Orthodox Christian (you might want to substitute "orthodox religious"), is not discussed directly but only alluded to in the sentence "Two hundred years ago this seemed a plausible alternative to the then orthodox idea that morality represented the decrees of a divine law-giver." The still-orthodox view, you may want to add.

Besides finding the religious perspective nearly invisible, students have difficulty in disentangling Rousseau's perspective from that of the contemporary scientist. Don't they both stress that man is a social being? And that ethics comes out of that social bond?

Ask students where the author starts to distance himself from Rousseau, and they may say, bluntly, in the sentence "Rousseau was wrong." Point out that the disagreement is registered earlier in the relation between the second and third sentences. That is to say Rousseau believed we were human first and social later. How did Darwin make that harder to believe?

You may want to tell students that "the social contract theory" is a familiar idea in political science, and ask them if they can figure out from the passage what it means. Singer's explanation that social contract theorists hypothesized a "Foundation Day," a one-time historical event, may be a bit wooden and misleading. By "the social contracts" political philosophers simply mean that at some point primitive people formed tribes when they learned they could benefit by trading some unrestrained freedoms for some group benefits.

An alternative: Have students brainstorm examples of ethical behavior. Then have them account for the causes of this behavior from the three perspectives.

Thus it may take some work, whether through writing or discussion, before you can establish the three perspectives clearly enough to see how ethical behavior might look a little different from the three angles — as law, as convention, as instinct.

The Expanding Circle is a book advocating animal rights. Ask students how Singer's discussion of ethics contributes to his general purpose.

A Social Science Option (p. 52)

We think the article by Alston Chase, despite its clarity for those already acquainted with the topic of saving the national parks, is very difficult reading for most freshmen. We also think it's wonderful ground for thinking about definition and political power.

If you've been working with summarizing skills in the earlier assignments, or even if you haven't, it's probably a good idea to ask your class to summarize Chase's essay before trying to work with it further. The summaries needn't be polished; in fact it's probably a good idea to tell your class that you hope their efforts at summarizing will turn up problems in their reading. They won't be able to summarize what they don't understand, but they will be able to locate more precisely the sources of their difficulties.

One subsequent line of approach is to ask students to compile a running list of terms that could use defining. The words needn't be those that are totally unfamiliar; on the contrary, advise them to look out for words, like *protection*, that seem to be used in some specialized or unusual way.

Why does *protectionism* have a negative connotation?

A key thematic sentence — key to the theme of definition as politics anyway — occurs in the final paragraph: "By defining intact ecosystems into existence, the Park Service created a rationale for continuing its policy of protection." Unpacking that sentence will take some work, but when students are able to do it, they will see what's at issue.

The scientific method is impartial, right? Ask students how this piece gives the lie to that idea. Who gets to decide what science is done? What do individual scientists get to choose or define? What role does governmental policy play in shaping scientific work?

Another way to frame the political question in terms of definition is to ask "What is a national park?" and "Who gets to say?"

You might ask your students whether they think the author is a Democrat or a Republican. You'll need to explain the economic analogy in "a laissez-faire approach." (Don't interfere with the economy = don't interfere with life in the national parks.) And you may want to explain the allusion in "voodoo ecology."

Voodoo economics was George Bush's characterization of Ronald Reagan's economic attitudes while the two were competitors for the Republican nomination in 1980. Translation in ecological terms: "Let the species slug it out; whichever victors emerge emerge victorious."

We have found that some of the best student writing about this piece takes a political perspective quite opposed to the author's. You may want to encourage students from the outset to treat the question of "What should a national park be?" as an open one. It's not an open question for Chase, who feels absolutely, with Leopold, that the function of a national park should be to "represent a vignette of primitive America." Do we need to agree with that aim? Who says so? *Must* we try to restore the parks to some prior state? Why not settle for protecting what's there now? Aren't we better off with relatively few rangers than a whole bureaucracy of ecologists, archaeologists, anthropologists, and other field scientists conducting "base line studies"? This is a point of view that can find plenty of fuel to work with in Chase's piece. There's no reason why the good critical thinking this piece helps to promote can't be turned back against Chase's own argument.

Reflecting on Definition

At the conclusion of your work with this chapter, it may be helpful to spend a few moments with the class reflecting on definition. Do students see definition differently now? What factors influence definition? How does meaning change and what does change mean? Who defines? What do we do with definitions? How do they influence what we see? In short, what do they make of all this? Often free-wheeling journal entries or scribbles on loose paper are the most effective way to work with such speculative musings, rather than within the more limiting constraints of a formal essay. It would probably be a good idea to have students save these reflections so they can use them as part of future writing as they explore other strategies during the course.

Defining, perhaps even more than the other strategies highlighted in this book, does not lead a separate academic existence. It merges and coordinates with the other strategies. In fact, this chapter can be used as a sort of prologue to the others: Defining as *serializing* is seen on page 112 and in the Biology Option; defining as *classifying* in Neisser's essay; defining as *summarizing* in First Pass #2 and the History Option; defining as *comparing* in Neisser's essay and throughout the Cases; defining as *analyzing* in First Pass #3 and the Philosophy and Social Science Options. Thus, the thinking that you ask students to do in this first chapter should seem somewhat familiar when they arrive at later chapters. Here, once again, our point is to underscore the recursiveness and interrelatedness of these observations.

Chapter 2

Summarizing (p. 57)

The intent of this chapter is to get students summarizing interpretively. Without undermining concerns for accuracy of representation, we want to encourage students to see that every summary *is* an interpretation, and we want them to think about how to employ summaries in service of their own interpretive efforts.

The chapter asks students to summarize a variety of texts — nonfiction readings, charts and tables, and narrative (both fiction and nonfiction) — and to consider both the differences and the similarities in the mental strategies they use to summarize different kinds of texts. Most important to the work of the chapter are the ideas that summary is always interpretive and that the purpose for which one is summarizing will determine the shape and content of the summary itself.

Because summary is a crucial academic skill and because this chapter contains several different kinds of texts, it may be helpful for students to do a good number of the assignments in this chapter. The whole class can work through the first part of the chapter — Cases and First Passes — and then do and discuss the Options individually, in small groups or as a class.

Before the class begins Working with the Strategy, spend a few minutes discussing what summary is and how and why writers might need to use summaries. Students will probably be able to think of a variety of examples, such as responding to test questions, taking notes on reading and lectures, writing case studies, repeating a conversation to another person, writing a letter to someone they haven't seen in a while, and so on. Move discussion immediately from the kinds of summaries different situations call for to the ways of deciding how to select and organize material for a summary. This conversation will lead naturally to consideration of the interpretation involved in deciding what to include and what to leave out. How does a writer decide?

Working with the Strategy

As students write and then talk about their summaries of the Lightfoot excerpt, consider how readers arrive at an understanding of the text. This assignment can be done in class, perhaps compiling a class summary on the blackboard after students have had a chance to write individually.

In trying to establish the passage's continuity, you might ask students to find key terms that thread themselves from paragraph to paragraph. The two most prominent: (1) *good* and (2) *idealized*. Note that Lightfoot doesn't define what she means by "good" — she simply wants to establish adults are unlikely to see what is good about contemporary schools because they are encumbered by an idealized recollection of schools in the past. This reading is thus one of many that anticipate a theme in the "Analyzing" chapter: The frame we bring helps determine what we see. Lightfoot seems to have been well aware of the problem, partly because she came to study high schools "after years of doing research in schools for very young children."

Ask students to consider the function of Lightfoot's paragraphs in her book. How might they take that into consideration in phrasing their summaries?

Ask students what they would like to know about the rest of Lightfoot's book. Some questions: What does she eventually define as "good"? Which schools did she study, and how did she choose them? Are good schools plentiful or rare?

When students work on a collaborative summary, they see firsthand how to discuss questions of meaning, how to stay firmly grounded in the text, and how to decide which issues of selection are most important. Armed with that knowledge, they should be prepared to move on.

Cases

Although you may want to assign this section to be read outside of class, some discussion of each case will be important. Many students believe summary is easy and quick: Raising the complicating questions will help them rethink their position.

A Case from Psychology (p. 59)

The summary which we offer on pages 60–61 of the alcoholism example from the psychology textbook (p. 59, ff.) is deliberately one-sided. We've gravitated to the structural features that lend themselves to parallel constructions (the four stages), bypassing the problem of what to highlight in the first two paragraphs. We encourage you to think critically about this summary. Our questions at the bottom of page 61 may help, but they may not be enough.

Consider asking your students to write a quite different summary of the alcoholism excerpt, altering the emphases. You might ask them to reduce the discussion of the four stages to a mere mention and stress the material in the first two paragraphs. Then talk about how this shift in emphasis alters the effect of the summary.

A Case from Sociology (p. 61)

The analysis of the reading on imprisonment guides students through the kind of thinking an active, questioning reader might do to make sense of a challenging text. You can begin to discuss adapting summaries to a specific context.

Direct students' attention to the use of quotation marks within the summary. Many students have difficulty interweaving relevant quotes from the original with their own remarks. Because appropriate quotation (and source documentation) is an important part of academic writing, a few minutes of explanation will be well spent.

Few students will read the discussion on pages 63–67 of the passage from *Society of Captives*, by Sykes, with much investment unless they've had to think for themselves about how to handle this text. So we'd encourage you to ask them to summarize this reading before going on to read our discussion of it.

On page 66 we ask students to note some of the differences between the summary that ends at the top of that page and the summary that begins at the bottom. The most striking differences, of course, are that the second version much compresses the first and then adds a second paragraph that begins to evaluate critically what has been presented in the first paragraph. But there are other differences too. The second summary lays out the three purposes in the first sentence, whereas the first summary drops them into sight one by one. The first summary, unlike the second, frames a question and then sets up Sykes as someone who offers an answer. The second summary implies a different relation between Sykes and the three purposes of imprisonment: In the first, Sykes "reviews" them; in the second, he "maintains" something about them. The second summary also emphasizes ("Most of the general public . . . Many people . . . Some people . . . ") what others think about the purposes of imprisonment, thus distancing Sykes from these opinions. The "we" in the first summary has the opposite effect. The second summary's opening paragraph is written with cues that the three points are going to be challenged in some way.

A Case from Folklore (p. 67)

With "The Singing Bone" we again invite you to pick up playfully and critically where we leave off. The summary on page 70, although it illustrates some points about the decision making involved in summarizing, is pretty flat. You might want to run through with students some of the animating purposes we suggest at the end of the first paragraph following the selection on page 70. Another approach is to try working with your class to develop assertions about this particular story or about folktales in general. For example, you might ask your students to analyze the role of the supernatural in this tale. So framed, the fairy and bone take on more emphasis in students' summaries, and the summary as a whole is made to support some general point (for example, that the role of the supernatural in fairy tales is often not that of an all-powerful force: The fairy's gift spear turns out to be no blessing and the singing bone may identify the murderer but it can't do much for the murdered man).

Another option is to offer to students the theory that since folktales have a common stock of characters and situations, some tales contain residual elements, features that seem to have little necessary function in the telling of the story (this idea might be offered in opposition to the impression that in tales so short every detail must count). In pursuit of this theory, students need to construct summaries that register the dubious details: For example, having mentioned in a summary the magic spear and the princess with whom the older brother is rewarded, a student can turn back on those details and claim they have little function — the story would work as well if the younger brother used a spear or his own (or his father's spear — think of the connotations) and if the older brother received some other award, an inheritance, instead of marriage to the king's daughter. Some such strategy and discussion should help you to make the point that contents of summaries shift to serve varying purposes.

If a number of students in your class seem to get interested in working with the folktale, you might consider letting them take their interest a little further. One strategy, borrowed very loosely from the structuralist approach of Vladimir Propp (see Carol Edwards, "The Fairy Tale 'Snow White'" in *Making Connections Across the Curriculum*, St. Martin's, 1986), is to ask students to list what they

they take to be key sequential elements in this tale that could probably be found in other tales as well. Here is such a serial list:

king
a threat (the boar)
younger brother
older brother
forest
inn
deception
murder
more deception
(marriage)
passage of time
disclosure of past sins
music
detective work
drowning
justice achieved
rest

Once the class has accumulated such a list (no need to be finicky about what constitutes an item), you might ask students to write another story preserving these same elements but changing details. Or you might ask your students to modernize it: Two sisters aspire to careers on Wall Street; or two brothers long to be rock stars.

First Passes

1. Summarizing an Argument (p. 71)

Stephen Morse's essay presents a number of typical summary problems for students to confront and analyze. They'll need to follow the development of the argument carefully, perhaps thinking in terms of the procedure they used when working with the Sykes piece on captivity. They should be encouraged to find the central idea of the essay and to try to state it clearly. If students read through the essay once, write for a few minutes about their understanding of its argument, and then go back through it orally to trace the ideas, they'll see yet another example of how close reading leads to effective summary.

Once they have understood the argument, they may profitably consider how they would summarize it if they were using it as part of an essay on the history of scientific discoveries. How would that summary be similar to and different from one that is part of an essay on the hidden dangers of "messing with" the environment? Or as part of an essay on the mysteries of the natural world? To make this task more concrete, you might want to divide students into groups and charge each with the task of writing a one-paragraph summary appropriate for one of these essays. Reproducing those summaries so the class can consider all of them should make for an interesting assignment in focus and detail selection.

To supplement this assignment and move beyond one-article summary, consider a synthesis of the ideas of this piece with those of "Sexual Reproduction" and "Eugenics" in the Defining chapter. How might students state an idea that draws upon the information in all three articles, and how would they summarize the articles to include them in such an essay? Asking students to summarize one more text should prepare them for synthesis tasks they'll encounter later in this book and in their other courses as well. In fact, they might discuss the sorts of academic (and nonacademic) situations that would lead them to do this kind of synthesis.

2. Summarizing a Table (p. 74)

This little assignment should make apparent how quickly summary shades into analysis, and how the latter gives purpose to the former. A literal line-by-line paraphrase of the table yields a string of dubiously related sentences: e.g., "Europe's percent of world trade declined between 1876 and 1960 from 66.9 to 51.4. North America's percent climbed from 9.5 to 18.4. The percent of world trade conducted by Central and South America moved . . . " The question, of course, is how to generalize about this data.

One strategy is to group the entries in some way, for example, Europe versus others: "In 1876 Europe accounted for two-thirds of the world's trade; by 1960, it accounted for only a little more than half. Other regions accounted for . . ." If students pursue this last line of thinking for awhile, you might want to redirect them by pointing out our clue about the title of the book. What point does J. Forbes Munro seem to be making with the chart? The 189.4 figure should leap out to make a point about the growth of African economies.

This table is so slender and the information it encompasses so vast, you might want to turn your students' attention to what the table can't tell us. What has happened in the last 30 years, for example? How were these statistics arrived at? Why might the "% change" be a misleading statistic? One student, who had read the Nkrumah and Fieldhouse passages in the "Comparing" chapter (p. 213), asked whether the European grip on African economies was masked in these statistics. Another asked how a table like this one constructed for previous centuries would have registered the economic activity of the slave trade. Would Africans captured by the Portuguese and imported to America show up as European trade?

3. Summarizing a Narrative (p. 75)

As students begin to tackle this task, you might remind them of the work they did with the folklore Case in this chapter. What similarities and differences can they find between summarizing a folktale and summarizing the narrative of a person's life? What do they notice about the organization of events — and about who selects and controls that organization — that might be useful? Are there, for example, patterns in the folktale that are absent from Roberto Acuña's life? A summary of Acuña's story may be sketchy at first, possibly as part of an ongoing reader's journal. Writing it will emphasize two important ideas: first, the connections between reading and writing that are central to this book and to students' learning processes and, second, the amorphous nature of thought and the helpfulness of committing ideas — no matter how sketchy and introductory — to writing. Students will do well to develop this habit. The questions on p. 75, particularly if answered in writing outside of class, should focus the reading and writing and prepare students to discuss the piece in class.

The first paragraph contains a central idea of the piece — and students may well realize that the first thing a person says about himself is likely to be important to his vision of who he is. The piece contains both a narration of events and Acuña's reflection on the meaning of those events to his life. Trace both strands, considering how the events of Acuña's life have shaped his perceptions and convictions and, conversely, how his growing awareness of the world has shaped his interpretation of the events of his life. The class may want to develop a quick time line on the board, combining important events with the related ideas to look visually at Acuña's life.

Having considered a narrative, think about how to put together a summary of it. Again, ask the class to consider a variety of purposes. For an essay on dawning social and political awareness, how would Acuña's story be told? As part of a speech directed to people growing up in similar conditions, how would the summary be shaped? In the context of an effort to convince others to support a political agenda, which items would be most important? How can a reader step back from the narrative and abstract the central themes of the experience? If students have attempted a rough summary first, they may be able to work in groups or as a whole class to talk about their assumed purpose and about how they shaped their summary. Alternatively, they may be able to construct summaries to fit one or more of the purposes above. In any case, they should see that their selection and organization of details will, first of all, be different from Acuña's and, second, be shaped by the purpose of the summary they're constructing.

Options

The issues in this section are the same as the issues in Cases and First Passes. How do we summarize accurately and purposefully? How does purpose shape the summary? How do summaries of expository prose, of tables and charts, and of narrative differ from one another, and in what ways are they similar?

An Anthropology Option (p. 81)

The passage from Conrad Phillip Kottak's textbook *Cultural Anthropology* is hampered somewhat by the author's effort to explain ideas at the same time he is crediting the ideas to particular anthropologists. Ask students which anthropologist is more central to the passage, Arnold van Gennep or Victor Turner. When they come around to saying it is Turner, ask what that suggests about how to frame their summary. You might ask each student to compose an opening sentence; then read and compare them.

Kottak goes to some trouble to get from "rites of passage" in general to von Gennep's three phases to Turner's focus upon one of the three phases, which he translates from marginality to "liminality." It's hard to see how this more specific term points to anything much more particular than the phrase "rite of passage" itself. And we've noticed that students who linger on this distinction between terms only get fouled up. The key point — at least it seems key to us — is to arrive quickly at the point that liminal states are reached not only by individuals but by groups.

When students turn to writing about a rite of passage from their own culture, they may cut their draft summaries quite substantially, a move that's probably worth encouraging. But if they've chosen to write about an experience involving group liminality ("communitas"), they'll probably want to preserve enough of their initial summary to indicate that not all rites of passage are group experiences. (You might ask students whether they feel our culture has any truly close counterparts to the individualized "vision quest" referred to by Kottak.)

Kottak's first and fourth paragraphs suggest a few possible topics, but most students do better if they choose their own example. Some topics that have worked well: college orientations; internships, particularly medical internships; some forms of group tourism; the graduation period of senior year in high school; junior year abroad; shared disasters. A few students have written persuasively about their entire college experience thus far as a prolonged episode of liminality.

If you'd like to linger with this piece, students might want to research and summarize some of the examples Kottak suggests. Personal accounts or anthropological studies will be most relevant. Students who do a bit of research might consider how they can most usefully summarize what they have discovered as part of an essay that supports or disputes Kottak's theory.

A History Option (p. 83)

Ask students to notice the title; the notion of loss provides a useful framework for their reading and summary of this article. In looking at issues of social stability and change, of social systems and how the individual fits into them, and of how the individual's place in society gets to be defined, you may want to look back at Terkel's *Roberto Acuña*. To illustrate a generalization about social change and its effects on individuals, how might these two essays be summarized as evidence? And, as the introduction to the piece suggests, how does all of this fit into or contradict students' notions of what it means to study history? Could they arrive at some general statements in response to that question that might usefully be illustrated by this piece?

An Economics Option (p. 86)

Many students find tables and charts daunting. Since they have already worked with two, though, those that follow should be less fearsome. This option provides a fine opportunity for drawing on student resources. Ask economics, social science, or business students to help the class by pointing out how to approach charts, how to interpret them, and what kinds of information they most often yield. Other students may need a bit of convincing to move beyond initial apprehension, but should respond to suggestions that the ability to interpret tables and charts is central to many fields of study and, indeed, to the ability to read a newspaper perceptively. The notion that charts and tables are also kinds of "texts" may be new to some students and is worth mentioning.

Group work with the charts and tables in class should help students get started on a longer at-home assignment that will also include consideration of the article. Even if all the work on this option is to be done in class, students should work with the chart and the table before they consider the print material. Otherwise, it's too easy to rely on the words and to lose sight of what the numbers offer in terms of understanding. The class should make sense of Kevin Phillips's comments, try to summarize them in a paragraph or two, and articulate his central point.

Then they may wish to try their hand at a definition of "the American Dream," noticing especially how the meaning of the phrase has both shifted and remained constant over time. Again, they'll be led to consider the way definition works and to think about the questions raised in their reflection on definition. Terkel's piece connects well here, too. What is Acuña's implicit definition of "the American Dream," and how does it fit with the material students are considering here?

A History Option (p. 90)

We suggest you ask students to scan this chronology several times and to try to construct several accounts of U.S. immigration policies. They might first try to characterize those policies in a general way. Is the pattern one of increasing constriction, or is that an oversimplification? Next students might try following thematic threads. What role do criteria like the following play as time goes on: health, labor, professions, nationality, total numbers, political concerns. Do some of these play increasingly greater roles than others? Students might then consider the perspective of Linda Perrin. From what vantage point does she seem to be thinking about U.S. immigration policies? What does she highlight? What further questions does her chronology raise?

Of what use would this chronology be if we were writing an essay about U.S. immigration policies in relation to Mexico? Why? What would we need to get started on such an essay?

As an exercise attached to this assignment, you might ask students to look at the data below. What relation, if any, can they find between these statistics and Perrin's chronology? What questions does a table like this one raise?

	1971–1979
Total Immigration	4,493,314
Total Asian Immigration	1,588,178
Total European Immigration	800,368
Breakdown of Asian Immigration	
Chinese	124,326
Indian	164,154
Japanese	49,775
Turkish	13,399
Other	1,236,544

(Source: Department of Justice, INS)

Another possibility for connection is to remind students of the distinctions between *refugee* and *immigrant* in the "Defining" chapter and ask them to consider which of the groups mentioned in this chart might fall into which category (definition and summary connecting to classifying). Another suggestion is to have them look at the Culture Shock pieces in the "Analyzing" chapter for fruitful connections. You may also want to discuss the historical context of the trends reflected in the chronology, particularly if some students are familiar with or can research a bit of history.

To move in another direction, you could ask students to interview immigrants in their own families or among their friends and friends' families about immigration experiences. Summarizing interview material presents a variation on the challenges students face in learning to be focused and selective in their summaries at the same time as they accurately represent their sources. These interviews might be discussed, shared, and then saved to become part of a longer piece of writing in connection with the Culture Shock pieces.

A Literature Option (p. 93)

Having worked on interpreting "The Singing Bone" and Roberto Acuña's life, students have thought about summarizing narrative. Nevertheless, "English as a Second Language" by Bernard Cooper is certainly more challenging because students must find an interpretive focus for their summary. To bring this point home, ask students to do a simple plot summary of the events of the story; looking at these should bring into sharp relief the barrenness of this approach. Without some interpretive purpose, such a summary is an empty exercise.

If students are going to work on their own to write about the story — which is probably a good idea — they'll benefit from some preliminary discussion of ideas around which they can organize. Language is one obvious starting point. Discuss verbal and nonverbal language, things that are and aren't said (both in and out of the classroom) and the ways in which those things that aren't said aloud are often said as audibly as those that are. Consider also the "dialects" of the story — the idiom of teaching and learning, the language of the Institute and of the interaction among faculty members, the language of the classroom, the issues raised by English as a second language and the use of Spanish, and the language of the gay community, as it is revealed in the interactions between the narrator and Ricardo. Focus on communication — and miscommunication — in all the settings included in the story. How does the theme of homosexuality connect to the second language theme? And, of course, consider the title; In how many ways is English a second language here?

Together, the class can work on forming some statements about these questions. Students need to see how the interpretation comes out of one or more close and careful readings of the story, out of thinking about how the details fit together, and out of their own perspective on the story. They need to realize that the summary actually becomes the details that they choose to support their interpretive statements and that simply retelling the story serves no useful purpose (except perhaps to confirm that one has read it).

After the class has explored interpretive possibilities, students can write individual pieces — either rough notes or short essays — in which they formulate a statement of controlling idea and develop it with appropriately written summary. Duplicating and sharing these in class should help students see not only the variety of approaches possible but also some successful and less successful ways of summarizing. If time does not permit sharing all students' work, representative samples will serve as well. Even two or three pieces can be very revealing; students will discover that others summarize differently than they do and that a range of thematic issues may be explored when they write about literature while the interpretation remains "true to" the text they're working with. As with defining, the notion of a "correct" answer is one students would do well to move beyond and the notion of careful reading and thinking is one they will do well to explore.

A Composition Option (p. 102)

Before reading Nancy Sommers's essay, students may spend a few minutes writing about their own strategies for revision. Ask them to do a brief journal entry or freewrite describing in some detail what *revise* means to them and exactly what they do when they revise. If time permits, have them interview a classmate to learn how another person thinks about and handles revising.

After sharing their observations, students should be ready to respond actively to Sommers's finding and her conclusions.

The best use of this piece, of course, is to draw students' attention back to their own writing and rewriting. Some students will already be engaged in the kinds of revising strategies Sommers attributes to adult writers. For those who aren't, the piece may induce them to look at their revising practices more critically and less cosmetically.

You might get students to play around with alternative summary strategies. For example, ask one group to summarize Sommers's review section in a paragraph. Ask another group to summarize it in a sentence. Compare the results. Does the group that wrote the paragraph have a better chance now of writing an accurate single sentence, or did writing several sentences produce a kind of distorition that makes a single, accurate overview sentence hard to achieve by this route?

Generate summaries composed by construcing a sentence or two each for the review, methods, findings, and implications. Generate others that employ a paragraph for each of these sections. Which is easier to keep coherent? Which is more likely to lead to a critical response to Sommers' article? Which is more likely to uncover "the dissonance of discovery" that Sommers sees at the heart of real revision?

Working from a fairly substantial summary of the article, ask students to write an essay about their own revising processes or those of their classmates. When they've drafted an essay, ask them to revise their summary — compressing, expanding, or adjusting it to suit what has become the purpose of their essay.

You might want students to work with this assignment in their journals or on loose paper, rather than in a more formal way.

For many students, Sommers's description of the revision process of experienced writers comes as something of a revelation. If you and they would like to continue the conversation — or return to it later in the semester — interesting supplementary material might include Nora Ephron's essay "Revision and Life: Take It from the Top — Again" (*New York Times Book Review*, 1986) and Mike Rose's *Writing Around Rules* (1985). If writing processes are a central focus of your course, you may want to send students on a library hunt to see what else they can find about revision. They can use their work with summary to help them report back to the class on what they have found and, perhaps, to expand their findings into an essay on their own revision process that makes use of summaries of several articles. If you prefer, you can save this possibility until the end of the course and ask students to employ the strategies they've learned — defining key terms, summarizing relevant reading, serializing the events of their own and others' revising processes, classifying and comparing revision strategies, and/or analyzing their own revision process in light of their own reading.

Reflecting on Summary

How has the work of this chapter shaped, confirmed, and changed ideas about summary with which students entered the course? Students need to think again about summary as interpretation — interpretation that must, to be sure, be true to the original text, but that is, nonetheless, a writer's perspective on that text. How, then, does a writer's purpose shape the selection process? And how can a writer be sure that he or she is being faithful to the text? Those two considerations are the central issues that students will face repeatedly in their academic careers, so they will do well to think about them in some detail.

Chapter 3

Serializing (p. 112)

Working with serializing can be tricky because we are apt to treat sequences mechanically, emphasizing matters of continuity — transitions, logical connectives, narrative fluidity — rather than matters of interpretation. If there's a theme to the chapter, it's that serializing is useful not so much for following directions as for seizing opportunities.

Students will, of course, be able to talk about how they have used serializing. Most will have followed recipes or directions for assembling or building something. Many will have written the frequently assigned school essay that gives directions for accomplishing some task: A partner then reads the essay and performs the operation, and the writing is evaluated in terms of how well it enables someone else to duplicate the task. In high school and college, writing lab reports requires students to serially describe procedures and results. But thinking of serializing as an interpretive strategy will be new to most students, we suspect.

Working with the Strategy

Before students begin the opening problem, you may want to ask them what they already know about the subject of water exchange between earth and the atmosphere: They may find it helpful to look at the figure. Then they'll approach the text actively, with some questions or assumptions already in mind.

This assignment may sound easier than it is. Despite the authors' claim that they are outlining a model of the hydrologic cycle, readers have to work to extract that model from the text alone (in their book the authors have a diagram to help them). In fact we need to work through a series of inferences. From the second paragraph we can infer from the approving quote of Ecclesiastes that the basic pattern is one from rivers to oceans. We can also infer from the sentence "Prior to the sixteenth century, it was generally believed that water discharged by springs and streams could not be derived from the rain" that today's scientists see rainfall as sufficient to feed springs and streams. Evidently the movement is from rainfall to springs and streams to oceans. Evidently, too, some water moves underground through rocks—since the sentence "The earth was thought to be too impervious . . . " is discredited by its context. This second paragraph should also make us aware that we need to account for the fact that ocean water is salty but rainwater is not. So to begin constructing the model from this second paragraph requires some detective work.

Fortunately for students struggling with paragraph 2, the quote from Leonardo in paragraph 3 captures the process in a few sentences. Students can fulfill the assignment simply by paraphrasing Leonardo. Whether or not they choose this strategy, however, the test for whether they have understood the main conceptual problem is whether their account of the cycle gets salt into the seas. Technically, the model has two prongs: Some rainwater flows directly into streams and rivers while other rainfall collects in springs, from where it seeps underground into rivers bringing small amounts of salt along for the ride; seawater, minus its salt, rises in the form of vapor and eventually falls as rain. The modern model, by the way, also accounts for the influence of vegetation in returning some water to the air.

These materials lend themselves to an alternative assignment: Trace the history of the idea of the hydrologic cycle. This seems at least as much the authors' interest as explaining the model itself.

You might ask students to contrast the historical reception of this particular idea to the receptions of the theories of Copernicus and of Darwin. Or make the contrast between Galileo's astronomy and Leonardo's hydrology. Why is one scientific idea more readily accepted than another?

Ask students whether they used the figure in conjunction with the text. Did they create one of their own? Which was more helpful? Why?

Many of the selections in this chapter ask students to work simultaneously with two examples of serializing. One may look at a process and another at the history of our understanding of that process. Or one may describe a sequence of events and the other the writer's own process of coming to understand that sequence. Considering the two strands — the model of the hydrologic cycle and the account of the historical development of this model — here and distinguishing between them, as students are encouraged to do in the questions that follow the text, should prepare them for thinking about the later assignments.

Cases

As you begin to look at the cases, ask students to think (and, perhaps, to write briefly) about why serializing might be useful or important. What does it help them do? What might they see differently when they use this strategy?

The three examples discussed on pages 115–117 illustrate a contextualizing more often available but often ignored. Head-on opinion questions which seem to back a writer into a corner can often be opened up to fuller contexts by thinking sequentially. For example, confronted with the stale yet volatile "Should capital punishment be outlawed?" a student can step away from the implied "State your opinion and now back it up with as many reasons as you can find" format, choosing instead a historicizing gesture:

> To ask whether capital punishment should be outlawed is to ask
> not only a moral question but a constitutional one. If the question
> means, as it seems to, "Should we as a nation allow some states to
> execute criminals?" it implies an attitude about the relationship
> between federal and state governments. We need to see such
> questions against the backdrop of the gradual erosion of states'
> rights. Since the 1930s . . .

As a classroom exercise, you might want to practice this kind of strategy for approaching questions, particularly if you spend time in class discussing how to take essay examinations or how to approach papers in other subjects. Suggest — or have the class collaboratively create — a list of typical questions that might lend themselves to serializing. Talk about the risks involved, the necessity of directing the answer to the question that was posed, and the possibility that a bit of research may be necessary to approach the question responsibly. You may also point out that finding a different kind of question within a question is a form of redefinition.

Stress the notion that serializing is a "vehicle for independent thinking" and that it allows readers and writers to "make interpretive judgments." The more actively involved students become in thinking about serializing in this way, the more likely they are to be able to use it productively in their own work.

A Case from Biology (p. 117)

The case of the biology lab report lends itself not to historical questions but to procedural ones. We ask students to compare the two versions of the Methods and Materials section, pages 118 and 119. But students usually will have trouble doing this unless they've struggled with the first one and felt some frustration. It will be hard to pinpoint the sources of frustration, so you might want to be ready to walk them through the first version, talking about the sources of confusion. A sentence like "This muscle stimulant forced the release of gametes through the gonopores of the animal at the aboral surface" is confusing primarily in its vocabulary. We get the idea: This sentence describes how egg and sperm were collected. But the sentence "Slides were prepared by applying Vaseline jelly to the slide in a circular pattern to raise the cover slip, thus protecting the gametes and forming a seal to prevent evaporation and desiccation" is confusing for a different reason: What is going on? What do the slides have to do with the concentrations of seawater just described?

The entire first paragraph of the first Methods and Materials section is confusing in another way: Because the sea urchins are the species under investigation, the student has first described the procedures for obtaining sea urchin gametes. In the actual laboratory situation students may have been preparing slides while lab assistants extracted sperm and eggs. But the effect of choosing to put this description first is to create the impression that the freshly gathered gametes must await the laborious preparation of slides before being tested. Readers feel the cumbersomeness of this description by losing track of the object of the experiment.

Here are some of the features contributing to the continuity of the second version of Methods and Materials:

The altered paragraph sequence.

The use of introductory phrases to indicate intention — "To test . . ." in the opening sentence; "to receive the eggs . . . " in the last sentence of that paragraph; and "To test . . . " in the final sentence of the third paragraph.

The use of transition words that manage our sense of passing time: "Next," "In the meantime," "When a minute had elapsed."

The highlighting of what is being tested — sea urchin sperm — by placing the key experimental moment at an emphatic point: the end of the second paragraph.

A reading experiment you might try: Before asking students to read this chapter, make photocopies of these two sections, and give the first to one half of your class and the second to the other. Explain to your class that a scientific experiment is structured by a hypothesis, a prediction that a scientist seeks to test by way of the experiment. Ask students to try constructing a hypothesis to fit the experimental procedures they have read. Read over these hypotheses and see whether a significant number working from the second Methods and Materials section are more accurate than the first. A good hypothesis will make clear that sperm are being tested for fertilization success at the various salinities: for example, "The experiment tested whether increased concentrations of salinity would decrease the ability of sea urchin sperm to fertilize eggs" or "Maximum fertilization success of sea urchin sperm was expected to occur at the normal level of ocean salinity." Do a higher proportion of those students working with the second example manage to grasp what the experiment is all about?

If you have worked on the summary chapter with your class, you might point out the similarities in using the two strategies. Just as straight retelling — this happened, then this happened — proved to be of little value in writing about literature, so simply listing events isn't productive. On the other hand, looking at events in terms of patterns or rhythms and of developing action may be a very productive strategy indeed.

Two Cases from Literature (p. 119)

The *Hamlet* example: You might point out that the student on page 120 is using serializing to help her define a problem worth writing about.

The Hongo poem. The rubric we offer on page 121 for writing about this poem may or may not work well. If you feel your students are merely filling in the blanks, we'd suggest you play with other ways to get them thinking about the movement of this poem. One nice way to get students thinking and writing with some attention to sequence is to ask how the vegetables of line 2 are different from the lettuce of line 20.

You might also ask students to classify the images of the poem in terms of the emotions they express. Which register affection, which seem neutral, which express anger or discontent? How do these images align themselves along the girl's walk?

In "An Interview with Garrett Hongo" (Alice Evans, *Poets and Writers*, September/October 1992), Hongo, a fourth generation Japanese-American from Hawaii, speaks of the poet's "need to portray the events of the world from our own point of view," to "speak as witnesses to historical events." To give further context for this poem, you might discuss with students the history of Japanese-Americans that it represents and show them how that history can add another dimension to the poem.

Cases from History and Political Science (p. 122)

The cases from history and political science present problems similar to those students tackled in their work with summary: how to select and order information.

As they work with the material on the Iran crisis of 1979–1981, for example, you might ask them to come up with a similar example currently in the news. Write up a simple sequence compiled over two or three days of news reports. Then call for more context. What issues of selection and omission emerge? News magazines and Sunday newspaper reviews of the week's news are fruitful sources of both events and contexts. Compare several accounts. How does the writer select? Does the selection make a point or communicate a point of view? If the events are ordered differently, is a different interpretation communicated?

The table on page 124, "Women in the Civilian Labor Force, 1890–1979": This is another section that could benefit from some preliminary work as an exercise before looking at the discussion we provide pages 124 ff. If you photocopy the list and ask students to write about it, you might work through three phases: (1) First ask students to write about the data, sticking only to the facts. (2) Then ask them to write interpretively, trying to account for the facts. (3) Finally, ask students to write about the limitations of the data. What else would they like to know to be able to interpret more confidently?

If your students have worked with the charts in the "Summarizing" chapter, they may be able to see here how summary and serializing can work together in interpreting and presenting conclusions drawn from tables and charts.

First Passes

1. Explaining a Process (p. 126)

One of the purposes of this book is to suggest new ways of conceptualizing familiar strategies and new ways of approaching texts, tasks, and problems in academic settings. Students need to see that the way they define a particular problem often affects the way they approach and solve it — and that a different strategy may lead to a new or at least richer interpretation.

This assignment can be tough to work with in a classroom setting because there's always someone who has seen the puzzles before or who solves the problems instantaneously — and the discovery is quickly infectious. It's probably best to give this as an assignment to be done at home.

It is also difficult to get students to report very precisely upon their failures and dead ends. And when they do devise solutions, they often describe them as bolts from the blue. Try to get them to be more specific about the mental conditions that made them ripe for discovering solutions.

Does solving one problem make it easier to solve the other? Do students feel they learn something about the nature of problem-solving in moving from one to another, or is each problem a whole new ball game?

Adams describes a number of solutions to the dot problem including crumpling up the page and sticking a pencil through all nine dots. But the most conventional solution is to (1) angle a line from the left edge of the upper left dot through the lower right edge of the lower left dot and then (2) extend that line down the page to a point where an upward diagonal line will now pass through the left edge of the lower dot in the central column and the right edge of the upper dot in that column, (3) and extend that line up the page to a point where one more downward diagonal will finish off the dots (a total of three lines). The impediment that most people report blocking this solution is a reluctance to go beyond the internal field of the nine dots, a constraint that is not imposed by the instruction.

Similarly, with the second problem, we tend to assume we need to preserve the image of an upward standing glass, and we also tend not to envision "half moves" of the matches. Once we allow that an inverted image of a glass is still an image of a glass, we usually see that we only need to slide the horizontal match half a length in either direction and then move the other, suddenly unattached match to its new position as a downward-facing side.

What we're calling *problems* in this assignment might better be defined as puzzles. One nice supplementary assignment to this one is to ask your class to brainstorm other types of problems — arriving perhaps at a classification of problems, or at least at an agreement that puzzles like these are only a subset of something larger. They are also very similar in their structures as puzzles. How do other puzzles vary?

Is there something we can learn from solving puzzles that applies to other kinds of problems? Our knee-jerk answer is yes, we can learn to examine our assumptions critically and playfully. But depending on what your students choose to identify as problems, that response may get some comeuppance. The puzzle model suggests problems with crisp, satisfying solutions — Ah ha! But your students may describe more painfully human problems — choices between dissatisfying alternatives, dilemmas, and decisions yielding no sense of resolution. Even those problems, though, may yield to a new approach, a reconceptualizing.

2. Interpreting a Text Sequentially (p. 127)

If the class has not yet considered "And Your Soul Shall Dance" on p. 121, you might want to take a look at that poem and the accompanying discussion before assigning "Digger Goes on Vacation." Students can look at the movement of this poem in light of Digger's (and the reader's) awareness of himself and his situation.

Writing a journal entry while reading the poem for the first time may help students here. If students write about their understanding of Digger as they work through the details of the poem, they should see both the movement of the poem and their own process of making meaning more clearly. How does the time context expand during the poem? How does the vacation fit into the larger context of Digger's life and personality? Around what thesis can they organize their interpretation? If your students have worked with some of the material in the "Summarizing" chapter, the necessity for an organizing idea won't be new to them. If they have not, you may want to spend some time showing them that a serial account of the poem without a central idea is nothing more than a retelling. If they organize their observations around a central idea — perhaps dissatisfaction, or the management of dissatisfaction — they'll see how the serial account becomes interpretive.

Though they will see that reading a poem is different from reading a newspaper or a table, they may also come to realize that looking at a text sequentially and placing it in a larger context can yield a useful interpretive framework.

3. Interpreting Events Sequentially (p. 130)

You may want to review the Iran hostage case (pp. 122–123) before moving into this assignment. Students can tackle this assignment individually or in groups, agreeing on a particular story to interpret. They need to see that sequence makes a difference — not only in how we understand the event, but also in our feelings about it — and that a different selection or sequence of facts will yield a different understanding of what happened and why.

We suggest working with international events because the chances are higher that these will gain from enlarging the historical context. But there's no reason events in the United States won't work as well. In recent years, for example, banking scandals and the collapse of savings and loan institutions have been much in the news. Bank failures due to too many risky loans are costly to all of us taxpayers, whose billions of tax dollars must cover the deposits, which are insured up to $100,000 per individual account by the Federal Deposit Insurance Corporation (FDIC). Continuing news stories give current facts but do not always explain the general background and implications. More context is lacking: Why were "bad loans" made? Were there no regulatory agencies overseeing bankers? Was corruption or fraud involved, or just greed? What will be the penalties for the bankers? And can it happen again? Of course the answers to many such questions won't be apparent from a single newspaper or magazine account either, but they will invariably give students more to work with. You may find that as students broaden the serial context, they raise more questions than these second sources address. You've discovered a good opportunity for a research assignment — particularly if your class is structured flexibly enough to allow such research assignments to emerge unpredictably. Such research assignments needn't be full-scale productions — it's enough that they are responses to a felt need. Used well, they may encourage students to develop some version of a manageable research procedure they can apply to other situations.

Our colleague, John Straus, asks his students to work comparatively from an evening TV news account and coverage of the event in the next day's newspaper. His students share what they have found with the class, and the ensuing discussion raises several important issues. As students discuss the difficulties they encountered in doing the assignment, they also consider the limitations of both TV and newspaper reports. Additionally, they look at the importance of context. Does a news article or TV feature present the trial of a serial killer as a series of gruesome revelations or as part of a history of the uses of the insanity defense? And what difference does that context make? Students raise questions about how much to include in their accounts: Is more information better? This question, of course, provides a fine opportunity to review the class's past conversations about how a thesis governs selection of information and to look at examples of thesis and support in students' own texts.

Options

Depending upon the needs of your students and the structure of your syllabus, you may want to select among these Options, either for whole-class consideration or for individual or small-group work. Students could choose based on their major or special interests, or you could assign groups to work with certain texts. In any case, it will probably be helpful to spend some time at the end of the chapter thinking about the issues raised by serializing and about the uses to which students might put the strategy in their future work.

A Biology Option (p. 130)

After reviewing the research itself, the purposes and context of the study on seal society, students need to look at the sequence of steps through which Jeanette Thomas designed and redesigned her research. How has she reconceptualized the problem during the course of the study? How did her increasing awareness of available technology help her overcome problems inherent in her early plan?

How did her findings lead her to expand and modify the research design? And how do her hypotheses emerge from her findings and from the events that shaped those findings? This account lends itself to an interesting comparison to the lab report in Cases (pp. 118–119). Students will notice the difference between a detailed account of research procedures following completion of an experiment, designed to enable someone else to replicate the work, and an account of ongoing research. This may be a good time to reinforce the notion that serializing means more than presenting a clear how-to or a chronological account with clear transitions.

Whether students write formally or consider the questions in rough, exploratory writing, they should consider Thomas's intellectual process next to their own as they read and make sense of her research. How does serializing shape their understanding of how knowledge is gained? Do they see ways in which the serial account includes the flexibility demanded by emerging research? On the other hand, was the actual process less linear than the serial account would suggest? If students take time to observe their own intellectual processes in solving a problem — not necessarily scientific — they might find serializing useful both to reveal the steps toward resolution and to discover that real, engaged problem solving is recursive in ways that a serial account may oversimplify.

They should also consider how different contexts would shape a serial account differently. A description of Thomas's research might take a different shape if the focus were on the intellectual processes of research, on the emerging knowledge of seal behavior, or on the ways that new technology facilitates research. To students who have worked with Summarizing, this discussion of context will sound familiar and may need only brief mention.

An Education Option (p. 135)

If students have not yet worked with the table in the Cases section of this chapter, you might want to take a look at that discussion before considering the table on characteristics of U.S. public school teachers. It's important for them to interpret the data, not simply to itemize what they see. Of course, the first step is to look closely at the data and notice the trends and changes. They might even want to keep a record of their strategy in dealing with the table — another kind of serial account.

To prepare for a more substantial essay, they can do a bit more research into recent trends in education to provide a fuller context for their interpretation. Or you can encourage them to keep their writing speculative and perhaps think of multiple causes for the phenomena they observe instead of settling for the first answer that pops into mind.

If the entire class is working on this Option, the students can work on the table individually as a homework assignment and then share their findings and their interpretations in class. Perhaps, the class can then work as a whole or as small groups to outline (or actually write) a newspaper or magazine article on the results of their investigation.

An Astronomy Option (p. 136)

Working with "How the Universe Will End" is another example of how serializing can help students enter scientific inquiry. The article reveals a developing understanding of the universe; all the data were not available at the beginning, nor is the answer fixed and static. Inquiry is an evolving process, and serializing can help us understand both how it happens and what has been found.

This assignment stresses the usefulness of serial strategies for coming to terms with lengthy readings. In perceiving this piece's serial segments, students come to a better understanding of the piece as a whole.

a. For *the closed universe*, use some of the material on pages 137–140. For *the open universe*, use some of the material on pages 137–140. For *the oscillating universe*, use pages 141–142.

b. The metaphors and the amount of James Trefil's text they frame:

The train moving toward the switchyard (from p. 137 on — it's still there at the end on p. 144)

If a ball is thrown up (pp. 138–141 "like the ball falling back to earth") a running film (pp. 142–144)

Note that these are structural rather than ornamental metaphors — they are used not for vivid effect so much as to give shape to whole stretches of subsequent discussion.

There's also the bathtub metaphor (p. 140) and the more general metaphor of "fire and ice."

c. Trefil, it's fair to say, favors "ice." Presenting his argument as a serial account is tantamount to writing a summary. Students should do justice to the way he frames the issue with the switchyard metaphor on (p. 137); the way he introduces the "closed" and "open" possibilities in on p. 138; the way he builds the case for the possibility of there being enough matter for a closed universe and shows how the question thus far must is unresolved (pp. 139–141); the way he moves through the closed and oscillating finales (pp. 141–142); and the way he chooses to end his essay with the film winding down in an open universe (pp. 142–144). The sequence of Trefil's material is itself part of the evidence of his admittedly tentative preference for "ice," but there's also the decisive, if qualified, sentence at the end of the "It is a fascinating thought" paragraph on p. 142.

Most of us probably read pieces like this with the dogged little question in the back of our minds "But what about me? Us?" One interesting way to reread this essay is to go over it with an eye for glimpses of humanity. Besides the metaphors, there's the little glimpse of ourselves reading this article when the oscillating universe brings us round again (p. 142). Then there's the science-fictionlike possibility Trefil attributes to Freeman Dyson of life evolving away from flesh and blood (p. 144). Of course the strongest human thread binding the whole piece is that of scientific speculation itself. The article is kept coherent, among other ways, by an almost celebratory tone that seems to say, "Isn't it amazing that the end of the universe is an issue is within the scope of our knowledge?"

An alternative question to the three we've asked on page 136: How does Trefil employ a sense of drama in an effort to keep us engaged in his article? Define what you mean by drama, and show it in operation by taking us through one or more dramatic stretches of the article.

A Literature Option (p. 144)

Your students may need a bit of guidance analyzing emotional and psychological associations before they begin to interpret the poem "Persimmons," by Li-Young Lee. If they have not yet looked at "Digger Goes on Vacation," a walk through that poem should help them see how association works. Before they write about the present poem, they can talk about it, with you or in small groups, to see how the images connect and how the speaker's mind links those images to events and feelings.

We've found that students' initial efforts to summarize this poem produce very awkward, transitionless chunks of paraphrase. But since students usually agree that they've had trouble, this problem can lead to richer ways of reading the poem. For if we look more closely at what prevents us from gracefully linking various moments in the poem, we discover that what takes us from sentence to sentence is associative rather than strictly sequential. Rather than gloss over the narrative discontinuities in the poem, students need to look for ways to register those discontinuities — and to look for some way of explaining how Li-Young Lee gets us from fruit to sex to his dying father. In short, the dissatisfactions that come with trying to summarize the poem can lead to stronger interpretive efforts to find a way of talking about the poem as a whole.

A few suggestions: Ask students to deduce a theme capable of taking us from episode to episode, for example, the theme of cultural differences, or the speaker's half-pained, half-whimsical relation to English words and their inadequacies. Better yet, simply ask students to follow the word *persimmons* through the poem, seeing what they can say about how it functions at each phase.

A History Option (p. 147)

Jane Tompkins's essay "Indians" points up the importance of rereading: Students will benefit from reading the whole piece at least once before discussing or writing about the questions raised at the beginning of the section. If class discussions have included personal experiences as sources of understanding intellectual strategies, you may ask them to think about some aspect or event in their own lives that they have come to understand differently as they have matured. If they look not only at the person or event they have chosen, but also at the reasons for change, and if they get very specific about those reasons ("I've matured" isn't enough, for example), they may be able to discuss how such changes in perspective take place. They don't need to share the personal experiences in class; sharing their own process of reflection should help the class come to see the rough outlines of the kind of intellectual journey Tompkins describes in her essay.

Description of an intellectual journey can be important to students' understanding of how a fully engaged learner conducts research. Often, students think of research as collecting — he says, she says, I think — rather than as an opportunity to challenge both the ideas and their sources: to bring different perspectives, criteria, and ways of seeing to bear upon an event, and to integrate their own knowledge of the subject. The parallel between the history of ways of seeing the subject and the writer's own intellectual journey provides another model and is therefore worth serious consideration.

This is a difficult article but fine preparation for the "Analyzing" chapter since it dramatizes in serial fashion how analytical lenses shape what we see. We also think that for people who can keep up with her account, Tompkins

61

dramatically illustrates an academic reader finding something personally at stake in her reading.

We encourage you to work with this exercise in groups. Ask students to delineate the key phases in Tompkins's thinking as it changes. Rather than simply listing readings, ask students to group them in significant clusters; simplify Tompkins's account by asking students to locate crucial shifts.

You might ask your students, at the beginning of the Option and later, what they think Tompkins means, at the outset of this long guided tour of her readings, by saying that "the present essay . . . doesn't have much to do with actual Indians" and "I ended up preoccupied with a problem of my own" (p. 148).

Paragraphs 5 and 6 encapsulate the overall structure of the essay. You'll want to help students discover this section without letting them settle for paraphrasing it. And what does it leave out?

Here's one person's demarcation of phases:

Childhood attitude

Perry Miller and the colonial point of view

Alden Vaughan on the humane encounter of Europeans and Indians

Higham and Jenkins on the violence of the encounter

Calvin Martin's ethnohistoric account from an imagined Indian point of view

Hudson's rejection of Martin's point of view

Axtell's reconstruction of captivity narratives

Heard's contrasting reconstruction

A primary source: Mary Rowlandson

Karen Kupperman's fresh ethnographic examination of English observers

Resolution (38)

If you can get your students to scratch out such a list, then see if you can get them to simplify it. Show how a serial account that treats a sequence of points like the eleven above would not be very effecitve if all the points were given equal emphasis.

Here is an additional question that may help students to frame some of the concerns of Tompkins's essay. In *The Chronicle of Higher Education* (Sept 27, 1989) David Thelan describes a new approach among American historians to the subject of memory: "Instead of visualizing memory as a full-blown representation of an objective reality that people retrieve from some storehouse in their minds, memory becomes an active new construction of a story from isolated associations, recognitions, and recollections . . . . People, in this view, fix their audiences very clearly in mind as they decide which elements to recollect, how to organize and interpret those elements, and how to make the memory public. They shape, omit, distort, recall, and reorganize a memory to fit changing contexts." What evidence do you find in Tompkins's essay compatible to this point of view?

Reflecting on Serializing

Serializing has various useful applications for the writer: telling what happened, describing a process so that someone else can replicate it or follow instructions, creating an interpretation or a piece of research. What are the differences between "how to" and "how I did"? How does serializing help create interpretation? How is it used to conceptualize a piece of research and then to modify and develop it during the process?

As students review their work with the material in this chapter, they should be able to see the kinds of flexibility serializing allows. The accounts of scientific and historical research show the development of the process — research is not fixed and static but is flexible and dynamic. How does serializing work with material that is already ordered and with material upon which the writer or researcher needs to impose order, to illuminate the material at hand?

In short, what does serializing enable you to do and to see? And, of course, what are its limitations?

Chapter 4

Classifying (p. 162)

Humans use classifying all the time as part of thinking; we constantly group ideas, people, and things according to schemes that may or may not be conscious. Through discussion, students can begin to become aware of some of their own systems for classifying information. We hope they will also, through the work of this chapter, come to see that they can challenge others' classifications, which often lie in the premises rather than in the conclusions of arguments they read or hear. Too often, students treat the systems of others as if they were reality rather than interpretive screens through which to view and order reality. They need to learn that they are free to counter with their *own* classifications, that classifying is an assertive, interpretive act.

Working with the Strategy

Students may need a brief explanation of metaphor before they begin to work with this collection. First, have them create a metaphor for their own writing process ("For me, writing is like . . ."); then they'll have their first thoughts available for revision after they complete the assignment. You might even try compiling and classifying students' responses before going on to look at what professional writers say.

In addition, remind students to be cautious using the "miscellaneous" category. They should first try to look in a different way at the metaphors, try another angle. If they keep a record of their work with the process, they'll be able to share in class not only the categories they've created but also the ways they arrived at those categories. Although it's likely to be difficult to record false starts and dead ends, encourage them to do so. The resulting record will be interesting; if they've worked with "Serializing," it should also be familiar.

Some practical advice about classifying will help students. In this instance, 18 quotations may be simply too bewildering to handle unless we find temporary ways of grouping them. Encourage your students to cluster the quotations: 1 and 17 use sculpting as a metaphor; 4 and 12 compare writing to giving birth; 3 and 14 employ sewing. As this clustering goes on, encourage students to look for more general catagories or clusters.

If the assignment works well, few of the students' category systems will be alike. Some will have more power than others, although it may be hard for the class to reach a consensus about which classifications are best and why. One of the best classifications we've seen so far employs a basic two-way division: "Some writers see themselves as recipients or vehicles; others see themselves as mechanics or operators."

You may want to hold onto the results of this assignment to use as part of a discussion of writing that began when students worked with Nancy Sommers's essay in "Summarizing" and will continue when they consider opening paragraphs from works of nonfiction later in this chapter.

After students have read the rest of the introductory material, engage them in discussion of times when people need to resist others' categories. Can they recall times when they themselves have done so? They may listen to or read samples of political speeches, replete with implied categories. Or they may think about their own perceptions of strangers. At the same time, they need to realize how often people categorize in everyday life as well as in academic situations. If they begin to consider both the strengths and the weaknesses of classifying, they'll be prepared to think critically about the material in this chapter (and, we hope, in the rest of their academic and personal world as well).

Cases

A Case from Sociology (p. 167)

The Talcott Parsons assignment that begins on page 167 is a tough reading of a type important to discuss with students: conceptually sophisticated material cast in academic jargon. English teachers sometimes dismiss Parsons because his prose is jargon-ridden; but students in sociology classes need to wrestle with that jargon and emerge with ideas.

To get anything out of reading this discussion and the sample student essay that follows, students need to slug their way through the reading. Have students work in groups and have each group specialize in one of the categories. Then have each student invent an example of an organization that fits that group's category. Writing separately, each group will tend to give much latitude to its category without much regard to Parson's system. With any luck, different groups will claim the same or very similar organizations to illustrate their categories. See if you can treat these competing claims as matters for class discussion and send students back to Parsons's text to see if its abstractions have gotten any clearer to handle. It's probably best not to pretend that the disagreements can be settled definitively — most organizations can be argued to fit each of Parsons's categories in some way.

Having worked through the reading as an exercise your students will be much better situated to follow — and perhaps to criticize — the deliberations of our sample student, pages 169–17. We think this is a good strategy for investing with some intellectual energy what otherwise would be a very dry reading experience.

In the student's essay, some of the best discussion occurs at the end of the first paragraph, "Parsons doesn't see his categories as mutually exclusive . . . " Once we realize that the categories not only overlap but are pliable, they can become fun to work with.

Again, emphasize the importance of exploring thinking in writing, no matter how rough. The process will help students both to work with difficult material and to see their own thinking more clearly. It may even help them look critically at Parsons's (or anyone else's) categories.

A Case from Public Health (p. 175)

As students begin to brainstorm possible categories to use to classify human diseases, they should also look at the interactive process of creating and testing categories. How do they see the information? Do they first work just with the definitions, or do they see immediately that the public health context provides a framework that needs to be considered? How do they decide what's useful? How do they keep their thinking flexible and not settle for the first idea that pops into mind?

Try to get students engaged enough in following the various sketches and false starts on pages 177 and 178 that the turnabout registers with some recognition: What are we doing and why? Classifying has the power to seem an end in itself — we need to keep coming up for critical air.

If you ask your students to step back from the structure of the assignment and to think for a few moments about public health issues, they may spot a joker. Nowhere does this scheme acknowledge the existence of heart disease. But how can that disease escape the classification scheme of broadly conceived public health discussion? Why might the teacher have excluded it? Should we? Ask your students how they might fulfill what this assignment asks for while registering their awareness of this major missing element. Make the case for treating the omission aggressively and giving heart disease a major position in the classification. How might students resketch the diagram on page 179?

First Passes

1. Applying Categories (p. 179)

The assignment that focuses on children's scribbles is a fine candidate for small group work. Ask students to try the assignment individually first and then to share and compare their results in small groups. Class discussion will yield interesting results. Have they read the passage as a way of establishing categories, or did they work first on their own? Did they find some of the scribbles more "advanced" than others right from the start? Were any difficult to categorize according to Kellogg's scheme? Why? How did they resolve the difficulty? Do they think there would be a difference in their attempts to categorize the scribbles if they could see the children produce them — perhaps even talk with the children as the drawings were done — rather than just looking at the finished product? If any of your students have easy access to children, they might even want to try this and report their findings to the class.

2. Creating Categories (p. 181)

If students haven't yet looked at the metaphors about writing in this chapter, now might be a good time for them to try their hands at that assignment. But doing the two back-to-back can also be uninspiring, especially if you use them similarly. We'd suggest that if you try both, you use one as the basis of brief writing and fairly full discussion; use the other as an assignment students are asked to perform independently.

With many quotations, classifying can become sheer drudgery; and it's easy to lose sight of any purpose in writing about *genius*. Encourage students to make distinctions and draw tentative conclusions. Don't let the classifying become an end in itself. After coming up with meaningful categories, they can use specific examples to test the adequacy of their categories, but even then the end needn't be to place every quotation in the master scheme. In fact, you might encourage your students, as one of the first teachers to use these materials did, to establish a "Miscellaneous" category into which to dump examples which seem unfruitfully problematic. For example, one of the quotations employs the word *precocity* rather than *genius* — students may simply want to sidestep any difficulties with using that term as if it were a synonym.

Something most of these quotations have in common is sententiousness. They are sentences which seem to have been offered up as quotable quotes, aphorisms. Perhaps there is something inherently pretentious about trying to tie down in a sentence a word we use for powers that are beyond us. Actually, this suggests one reasonable basis for classification: statements which seek to demystify genius versus statements that insist on its mysteriousness. Another basis for classification, one perhaps too dependent on historical knowledge, is to decide which are statements of people — like Edison and Goethe — who are themselves consdered to be geniuses. Incidentally, it's possible to build into this assignment a small research component. Make each student responsible for researching one of the people quoted (better do a little pruning first). On what basis might each of them have something to say about genius?

If you have been speaking about figurative language in earlier assignments, encourage students to develop a classification along metaphorical lines:

I.   Nonmetaphoric statements
II. Metaphoric statements

How might these general categories be subdivided? Do the metaphors for genius sort themselves intd types?

Other observations may prompt some categories, if prompting is needed: (1) Which statements say "Genius is . . . "? What do the others do instead? (2) Which statements connect individual geniuses with their societies? Which of those relate genius to public disapproval? (3) Which writers see genius as something already there? (4) Which see it as a matter of combining two or more crucial factors?

It might also be worth pressing some of these quotations for how little they say. Lowell's resounding claim, for example, can be reduced to saying "Works of genius are recognized as works of genius."

If a full-blown classification of these quotations seems daunting for your students, you might want to have them work with a theme. Have them select a vein of quotations according to a theme. For example, ask students to write a short essay arguing either (1) that genius is merely a matter of hard work, or (2) that genius is a matter of inspiration. But be forewarned if students attempt to write such an essay merely by stringing together quotations, the resulting essays will read oddly, as a mere tissue of quotations. Ask what other kinds of material, besides supportive quotations, they would need to write an effective essay.

3. Reevaluating Categories (p. 184)

The assignment on Robert Redfield's "Little Communities" employs categories in a different way than the other assignments in this chapter. The categories are separate and unequal. They are not subdivisions or branches of a single trunk. Each category is a separate criterion in its own right. Taken together, the four categories — smallness, distinctiveness, self-sufficiency, and homogeneity — constitute not a classification system but a kind of weighted check-list: How well does Community X conform to category A, B, C, D?

Before your students try applying the categories, you may want to talk with them about the difference between the classifying they'll do this time and the classifying they've doen in the preceding assignment.

Here again the notion of a continuum can be helpful. None of the communities conforms perfectly to the abstract definition of a little community, but some conform much more closely than others. Discussion of which communities are "littler" than others hinges partly on which criteria are weighted the most heavily. Because Redfield does not tell us which criteria are most important, we are left with much latitude for debate. Most students, if they arrange the communities along a continuum, arrive at the following judgments:

Little Community	**Least Like Little Community**
Hutterites Hualcan The Iks	Springdale The Vice Lords

The *Hutterite* community is small, distinctive, and homogeneous, and its economy, despite some outside trading, is essentially self-sufficient. Moreover, though this is not one of Redfield's criteria, they self-consciously define themselves as a little community, purposefully bounded off.

The village of the *Hualcan* is small and distinct, the villagers are quite homogeneous, and their economy is relatively, though not absolutely, self-sufficient. If it's a question of distinguishing the Hualcans from the Hutterites, though, their insularity seems relatively accidental. But to distinguish these two by degree is probably to quibble.

Some students may classify the *Iks* as even a closer fit to Redfield's generalized description of a little community. Their village is small and certainly distinct, and the Iks are homogeneously nasty. They also have little contact with an outside economy, although it's hard to characterize starvation as self-sufficiency. They may have fit the definition more closely when they were nomads. The more important point in writing about the Iks, we think, is to see that regardless of how well they conform superficially to Redfield's definition, they run counter to the whole ethos informing Redfield's study. As such, they present a problem: If the Iks are a little community, why should we be concerned that we no longer live in little communities? Of course it's possible to see the Iks as a little community gone awry, its problems not generated from within but imposed from without by the Kenyan government.

Springdale helps to draw the distinction between a small town and a little community. Only to a degree is it distinctive, small, or homogeneous, and it is no more self-sufficient than any other town linked by the American highway system. The *Vice Lords*, whatever else we might want to say about their life as a group, do not correspond to Redfield's definition of a little community, or of a community at all. They are small, and they may be homogeneous (although that's not clear), but they are not distinctive in that their boundaries are vague and their membership fluid. And there is no question of self-sufficiency. Each member has a life apart from the group. Working with this particular description should encourage students to see the need for some sort of wholistic rather than itemized judgment. Having two out of four criteria needn't count for much. Working with the Vice Lords example may force us to consider which categories are most crucial to the definition.

You might consider letting students play with an argument counter to the thrust of Redfield. Let them develop the argument that little communities do *not* minister to basic human needs — that little communities are accidents of history and as units of living they are expendable.

As with the other assignments in this chapter, there is a danger of the classifying becoming an end in itself. A question to keep in sight: What does Redfield think we gain by defining little communities? A question to let surface: What else can we discover? One discovery, for example, may be that students find other, better questions to ask: What is a community? What are the features of a healthy community? Where there is no community in a carefully-defined sense, what takes its place? What forces erode communities? What is the relation between community and conformity? Between community and hostility? Between community and self-definition? What benefits do communities confer? What prices do they exact? One way to do this assignment is to go through the applications of Redfield as an exercise, and then create a fresh assignment that asks students to classify these groups on some evaluative basis of their own choosing.

Options

Depending on the needs of your students, you can encourage them to choose among these Options, or you can assign Options that fit well into your syllabus.

An Anthropology Option (p. 189)

A brief discussion of body language — what it means and how it has been studied — will help students understand what they are to do before you send them out to observe and collect data on the body language of college students. For a concrete example of specific detail in description, refer them to the Penelope Eckert excerpt on page 196. Ask them, either before or after their observations (or perhaps at both times), what body language reveals. Why is observing and classifying it useful?

This assignment can be taken in several directions.

As an exercise in classifying, much will depend upon whether a writer confines herself to a single vantage point (a school cafeteria, for example) or ranges among several (a bookstore, a gym, classrooms).

This assignment can be converted to an exercise in the generation of details. Many students will bring back skimpy initial descriptions. Ask them to return to the scenes of their observations to thicken their descriptions. Or better yet, have them return to these places equipped with hypotheses generated by their initial visits. For example, some observers might predict, based on their initial observations, a difference in style between male/male encounters and male/

female encounters. Establishing the differences persuasively will involve the inclusion of telling details.

Alternatively, you can get students to write from the outset in great detail, asking them to record their direct observations in as much detail as they can and as rapidly as they can. Then initiate a second phase of the assignment that asks them to produce categories for their observations. Finally ask them to do a second round of observations with their categories in mind, asking themselves how well they suffice to describe the behavior they see.

This assignment also lends itself to group work, either in small groups or collectively as a class. You might send each student to a different spot on campus, for instance, and then when the class reassembles spend some time synthesizing the information gathered, trying as a group to impose some form on the separate observations. Talk about the frustrations of trying to do so. What variations in methods and perceptions make it hard to generalize? Perhaps as a class you can agree on a strategy for refocusing and regularizing the study. The imprecision attending the effort of thirty people to observe something as unspecific as "body language" might be supplanted by a decision to study "hand gestures," and the class might try to equip itself with a fundamental vocabulary of such gestures. Then back to the field for a fresh set of observations. Perhaps the categories arrived at could be used to test a hypothesis. Does the prediction hold up that the hand gestures used to communicate in the gymnasium are different in both kind and frequency from those employed in the corridors of school buildings?

An Economics Option (p. 190)

One key to this assignment is in getting students to read Leonard Silk well. Asking students first to paraphrase this passage is probably a good idea, but we've noticed that the paraphrases often remain very close to the language of the passage, masking difficulties of comprehension. One suggestion is to ask students, along with their summary or paraphrase, to work with one example. What is the fundamental difference between the two categories Silk offers? For example, how would someone looking at the price of gas or the price of beef explain fluctuations in price?

If your class as a whole is having difficulty, we'd suggest you work through an example of your own invention. Or borrow this one: Economists in the first category, who see economic outcomes as the results of many individuals pursuing self-interests, would explain a rise in milk prices in terms of the individual choices: consumer decisions whether or not to purchase milk raise or lower the aggregate demand for milk; milk companies set their prices in relation to their competition and what the market will bear; individual dairy farmers decide whether or not to invest in more cows based on their calculations of how soon they can expect to make a profit. The economy consists of a multitude of such decisions. Economists in the second category would say that individual decisions at the level of the consumer or dairy farmer play little role in the economy. The price of milk is affected only by the policies of a few conglomerate dairy companies, or the subsidy policies of the federal government, or changes in tax structures, or the actions of banks tightening or loosening interest rates of loans.

The examples you choose to work with can color the perception of the issues. How might the climate of discussion alter if the example were auto insurance rates or college enrollment? One way to generate a good discussion of Silk's two categories is to ask each student to develop in a paragraph a single example like the one above. Then ask the class to pool examples. Which easily illustrate Silk's dichotomy and which do not?

The discussion of the term *model* in the introductory section of the "Defining" chapter might help to gloss Silk's use of that term in his final paragraph.

Having worked in some detail with the Silk passage should prepare students for reading the other passages attentively. That passage becomes, in effect, an analytical tool. If the tool still feels a little cumbersome, you can make it more manageable by asking your students to phrase a Silk-inspired question to ask of the various texts. Here's one: Does the writer favor government intervention in economic activity? If not, he's in the first camp. If so, the second.

You may want to stress that the brevity of these passages means that we are being exposed to only a small portion of each writer's thinking. While it's often possible to make effective generalizations on the basis of a little evidence, you'll also want to point out the wisdom of tentative judgments.

Here is one person's application of categories, with a few notes on the passages. It may be a good idea to try to place the various writers on a left-to-right continuum, particularly since there may be interesting disagreements about who is to the left or right of whom. This exercise, by the way, offers a good opportunity for students to think about those two political terms — left and right —in an economic context.

For Government Intervention	For Laissez-Faire
(Silk's second category)	(Silk's first category)
Gorz Schumacher Thurow	Kahn North and Miller Friedmans

Friedmans.   There is little room for argument in the placement of the Friedmans. Almost any sentence yields evidence. The ubiquity of the word *free* is one indicator, but so are sentences like "And what produced the miracle? Clearly not central direction by government" and "They got little assistance from the government. . . . They encountered little interference from the government."

Thurow.   The emphasis is on planning. The second paragraph, by emphasizing *deregulation,* may seem at first sight to be advocating a hands-off policy, thus sliding Thurow into the right-hand column. But the subsequent paragraphs should bring us back to this one to correct that possible misreading: Deregulation is a public, large-scale decision and a device of control within the power of the government. One clear tip-off is at the start of the third paragraph: "Solving our energy and growth problems demand (*sic*) that government gets more heavily involved" and the remainder of that paragraph.

Kahn.   Kahn's position seems more middle-of-the road. On the one hand, "in our own country the free market system normally operates well without additional guidance from the central government." On the other, "a wise government can improve both the choice and rapidity of adjustment or innovations by intelligent, sensible, and skillful intervention." But juxtaposing these two quotes is misleading, and you might ask your class why. Kahn so heavily qualifies the case for government intervention that the net effect is an endorsement of a hands-off policy. It's very much worth asking students to point out sentences that convey the two parts of Kahn's attitude while also converying their relative emphases. There's a case perhaps for putting Kahn in a category of his own, apart from some of the extremes of the other positions.

Gorz. This may be the most difficult passage to work with because its tone is hard to judge and its scope seems so different from the preceding paragraphs. It's hard to decide whether Gorz is advocating something or merely describing. What's safe to say, however, is that for him the notion of individuals or even groups being "free to choose" is misleading: "Self-management is meaningless."

Gorz is writing far from the left, but it's only an acquaintance with his work as a whole that enables us to say so. We think that students may legitimately infer from the vehemence of this passage that Gorz is so outraged by the vast institutions that shape our lives (even shaping our perceptions of our needs — that first paragraph will take some unpacking) that he's advocating a return to the laissez-faire of yesteryear. Actually, he would say that you can't get there from here. One glimmer of what Gorz advocates can be seen in the third paragraph: "What is needed . . . " In other words, according to Gorz, we don't have much freedom in our economic lives, but what we do have should be exercised to help shape those institutions which will be making our decisions for us.

This reading, we know, is an example of leadenly written academic prose, but it's also fairly representative of the kind of academic wading students will sometimes have to do.

North and Miller. This is also a difficult reading to characterize. On the whole, North and Miller are proponents of letting the invisible hand of economic market forces have its way. Students may want to see the passage as sheer description: Here's something that happened in the 1970s and a forecast that the authors made at the time; the passage doesn't seem to lend itself to Silk's categories. But a close reading of the first paragraph for loaded language should alert students to North and Miller's leanings. The price of petroleum after 1973 "was not allowed to rise." We experienced shortages "because of those controls." There is a "maze" of regulations preventing the operation of the free market. The role of "old oil" has "discouraged" the production of oil that would eventually bring down oil prices. Prices are "artificially" low.

Schumacher. Individuals acting in their own immediate self-interest will only lead to the squandering of a fine oil supply. Governments and their institutions are capable of acting upon long-term interests. The long-term problem requires "concerted action."

These last two passages can make for an interesting comparison as a separate assignment. What do Schumacher and North and Miller agree upon? How do their analyses differ? Do they disagree on fundamental facts? Do they disagree about how the economy works? Do they agree that there is an oil crisis and that something must be done?

A Literature Option (p. 196)

Here again we'd suggest that what matters is not whether students can create a comprehensive system for classifying the paragraphs (although that can be fun to attempt); it's whether the activity of classifying leads to interesting observations, distinctions, questions.

The number of quotations is meant to provide a complex field of operations, a testing ground for generalizations, ample turf for making discoveries. Students shouldn't make the creation of an inclusive system an end in itself. Nevertheless it's effective to use particular examples to test categories that students choose.

Students absorbed in efforts of classifying are apt to be irritated when they run into problematic examples, paragraphs that don't quite fit their scheme of things. They will need encouragement to see those problems as something to work with and highlight.

Some random observations about these passages:

You might note the willingness of nonfiction writers to speak of "this book" and, more generally, of announcing their intentions.

You might ask whether absolute distinctions are always possible. For example, how is the opening paragraph of Bagdikian different from an opening paragraph of fiction?

Which paragraphs both announce a topic and indicate a stance toward that topic? (In other words, which set themselves up clearly in terms of an an analytical frame?)

You might advise clustering as a strategy. What does the paragraph by Cox et al. have in common with the Jacoby paragraph? What are the similarities between the Bagdikian and Gere paragraphs?

Note the number of paragraphs that do something we might call "setting the scene."

With the Owen paragraph, how much is lost if we miss the allusion to "The rich are different from you and me"?

As a possible follow-up, show students the advice that a composition handbook (or several) provides about how to begin an essay. Compare those pieces of advice with these actual texts and with the categories students have developed. You might even include beginnings of your students' own essays, both those written in your class and any older pieces of writing they can unearth. What effect do these expanded examples have on the category systems? Do they fit into the categories students have already developed, or do they demand additions? Do they call any into question? Do they make distinctions between beginning and professional writers?

If you'd like to focus more on writing strategies, look at the expectations each kind of beginning sets up and the effects each has on readers. How might students choose among these strategies to widen their own repertoire of openings? If students are working on an essay when you consider this assignment, ask them to try several alternate openings and discuss how they might choose among them. And, if you ask your students not to begin their writing with an "In this essay I will" kind of opening, you might want to tackle head on the many writers in this assignment who actually do use that strategy. Talk about the demands of different kinds of writing. When might students need or want to use this beginning? And are there ways to vary it to make it interesting instead of offputting?

If you or your students would like to investigate opening strategies even further, "Rhetorical Beginnings" by Louie Crew (*College Composition and Communication,* October 1987) will be useful supplementary reading. In this piece, Crew compares "the rhetorical opening moves of twenty professionals with those of twenty rank student amateurs." His conclusions and the categories he discovers are revealing, and the article would make a good pairing also with Sommers's piece in "Summarizing."

An Art Option (p. 204)

This assignment works best, we think, when it is left open-ended, at least at the outset. Students will react to these images in unpredictable ways. In the spirit of this chapter, you may find it interesting to classify your students' initial classifications. How varied are they? Upon what basis do they choose to classify?

Since we've titled the assignment "Images of the Human Form," some students will choose to divide the images into "realistic" and "nonrealistic" or some such pair of binary opposites. This may not be an especially fruitful classification, particularly if students wind up with one or two images in one category and the rest in the other. Students may need to be persuaded to make distinctions among the pieces they lump into one unwieldy category. If, on the other hand, they place something like "The Persian" in a category they label "realistic," you'll want to press them on what they mean by that category.

Students doing this assignment may express frustration with a lack of vocabulary for talking about art. You may be able to work with this frustration a little. Ask them to be as specific as they can about what they would like to be able to describe better. Look at the images together. Have the class collectively articulate a serviceable vocabulary.

You may eventually want to let students use their initial efforts at classification as a prewriting device for another sort of essay altogether — perhaps a comparison or an interpretation of a single artwork. Encourage students to take their essays in directions suggested by the strong points you and they discover in what they write. If you let the initial acts of classification serve merely as a starting point, you may also find it interesting to see if the resulting essays retain vestiges of the initial writing. You might even ask students after they have written essays to comment on how, or whether, the effort of classifying influenced what they eventually chose to write.

We've confined this assignment to images from a single era so as to encourage generalizing: not only "These works of art of the 1920s may be divided into several types . . ." but also "These works from the 1920s suggest that this was a time of . . ." These latter generalizations, we realize, will be much shaped by our own no doubt idiosyncratic selection of images. Let us mention two biases of which we are aware. We've chosen a high proportion of etchings and drawings — pieces that lend themselves to black-and-white representation in this textbook. Perhaps allied to this tendency is a preponderance of caricatures and grotesques. Both of these tendencies, it's fair to say, are capable of warping a viewer's opinion of art in the 1920s. We think it's a good idea to try to elicit this objection from students, particularly since it's an objection portable to any anthology they meet: How representative is this sampling? What does it leave out? What distorted impressions does it leave? What might a fuller context teach us? In fact, since we see the cultivation of this sort of suspicion as one of the critical aims of this book, you might try a research antidote. Make a portion of your class responsible for researching the artists represented here. Are the selections we've chosen really representative of their work? Of their work in the 1920s? Ask another portion of your class to research the work of *other* artists of the 1920s. Do these alter the picture? How were they selected? Have both groups of students file short reports to the class.

If your school has an art gallery or museum or a regular exhibit of students' art work, or if the surrounding community has its own museum that is accessible to students, you may want to send them out to look at some actual paintings and to repeat this exercise on a larger scale. In fact, if you or they are interested, the museum or gallery visit might be the subject of a longer paper to follow this assignment. You might ask students to focus on a special exhibit, to study a group of art works that you specify, or to find their own categories. If there is time to talk about the results of this excursion, students may be able to share new ways of seeing as they discuss their perceptions of art.

A Legal Studies Option (p. 210)

We've included this essay not only to broaden the discussion of classifying but also to spark reflection on the process. Ask students in what ways this essay is about the process of classifying. And how has the author used classifying in writing the essay? How does the essay address the question of the dangers of rigid classification? If you ask your students to summarize the essay, they can discuss how summarizing and classifying can work together. And they can extend Minow's categories to include concrete examples from the newspaper, the news, TV law shows (fictionalized though they may be), and examples from other areas of their own experience. Their writing, then, can become not only summary but also response that looks critically at the ideas Minow proposes and at the ways in which our everyday language embeds categories of which we are often unaware.

Reflecting on Classifying

It's important to get students to recognize the pervasiveness of categorizing in our thinking, to realize that categories both help us to see as well as impose limits on what we see, and to become willing to challenge the categories that underlie the arguments they confront in academic and personal life. Ask them why people create classification schemes. Categories help us to make meaningful connections, to avoid seeing each instance as separate and unconnected to others. They help us make sense of our experience.

Ask students to observe their own thinking for a few days and to record in their journals ways in which they see themselves using categories. Ask them to look outside themselves at what they hear and read to see how others classify experience. They can look at discussions of different types on television shows, at politicians who distinguish among groups of people and policies, at people who classify children's behavior (Piaget, Brazelton, Kohlberg, Gilligan, to name just a few) in order to draw conclusions. Whatever their own fields of interest, they should become familiar with the systems used to classify information and the categories that define a way of looking at data.

Look again at Neisser's (pp. 11–13) definitions of intelligence and the categories he uses. Review Studs Terkel's Roberto Acuña narration (p. 75) as he categorizes the experiences of his life and reveals how he has arrived at his current ideas. Reconsider the story "English as a Second Language" (p. 93) to see again how students created categories in order to interpret the story. How did Thomas classify seal sounds (p. 131) in order to arrive at conclusions about their meanings? In Tompkins's account of her work with Indians (p. 147), how does she use categories to group both ways of seeing Indians and her own process of understanding? Of course we don't expect that your class has read or discussed all these pieces. But this seems a good place to review some of the work they have done so far to see how classifying works with the other strategies they've considered.

You'll probably also want to ask about times when classifying is not helpful. When the categories are so broad, for example, that they offer no useful insights or when classifying becomes synonymous with labeling and stereotyping, then the usefulness of the strategy needs to be called into question. Students need to see that any strategy that helps us think effectively can also get in the way or help us avoid thinking if it is misused. They may already have considered this possibility if they have talked about the summary that retells what happened but serves no purpose, or about searching the dictionary for a correct definition without considering context, or about applying a label to a group of people without thinking about or looking at individuals.

Ask students to think about and discuss the "sorting" categories from their own fields of interest. What theories help people in their field understand data, behavior, events, etc.? What categories emerge from those theories? Do students know enough about the history of the field to be able to look at how those theories and categories have changed over time and what difference the changes make? When the categories shift, how does our understanding change? This familiarity with the language and classifying schemes of a few fields will help prepare students for their work with Chapter 12 of this text — or, if they're unfamiliar with these issues, will give them a set of questions to ask in other courses as well as in their approach to later chapters of this text.

As students continue to work with this text in your course and to think about their other academic work and their everyday experiences, urge them to look carefully at the categories that have been created for them and that they are expected to apply, as well as at their own creation of categories to understand their experience. This awareness will certainly help them think more critically.

Chapter 5

Comparing (p. 213)

In asking students to think about and practice comparisons, it's hard to avoid the impression that comparison is a form rather than an activity or an attitude. There's a danger in working too hard with the assignments of this chapter, grinding out comparisons rather than letting them develop spontaneously in unanticipated ways and in other contexts. Although students will learn they can structure an entire piece of writing as a comparison, it's more important for them to feel they can call up comparisons quickly and playfully, then drop them as their purpose is served. We recommend lightness of touch as you move about the chapter, particularly with the early assignments: Be willing to sacrifice completeness for quick flashes of insight.

Working with the Strategy

As students begin the introductory problem, take a moment for students to scan the titles and brief notes that describe the sources of the excerpts. Ask what they expect to read. Later, consider with them the attitudes toward workers that the excerpts reflect. How are workers perceived by the managers quoted in the excerpts? How do their perceptions affect management policies? And what do the authors seem to feel about these policies?

You may want to discuss the assembly line model of industry, which breaks tasks down into their smallest motions so that those who perform them become interchangeable. (Refer to the discussion of *model* in the "Defining" chapter if your class has worked with that section.) Consider the alternative perceptions of workers that the articles suggest. Depending on how one perceives workers, what does it mean to manage? What kinds of training would be appropriate within each model of management? What responsibilities are inherent in each? How are workers expected to behave? To feel about the work they are doing? How are workers represented in the media? Are these representations accurate?

Students' observations of the issues raised in both readings should help them frame their comparison. They can organize around a question: How do the authors perceive workers? What does a manager do? What are the implications of the viewpoints expressed? How do students' own views of the workplace, of workers, and of management styles affect their readings of the two articles?

After they reflect on the questions in Thinking about Thinking, ask students to work in small groups to compare their responses to the questions — and to see another use of comparing.

These observations may lead naturally to consideration of the remaining introductory materials. Students might consider why comparing can be a useful strategy and what they can do with it. In what contexts can they imagine using comparisons? When would comparisons be helpful?

Cases

Two Prose Excerpts (p. 219)

The Frankl/Ellis comparison: On page 221, we solicit dissatisfaction with the paragraph that ends at the top of that page. Students may be slow to take up this invitation, feeling that the paragraph reads "fine." In this case, we recommend moving on quickly to the next paragraph and then comparing the comparisons. Students usually see fairly quickly that the first comparison loses the forest for a few trees. To treat the concentration camp obliquely, equating it merely with "real life" as opposed to the "fantasy" of the Ellis passage is to step past the emotional quality of the passage.

Reconceptualizing the comparison between these two passages asks students to reconsider their first thought and try to find a more productive approach. (If your class has talked about the puzzles in "Serializing," they may notice a similar theme here.) This kind of flexibility, or willingness to think again instead of stopping at the first thought, is often hard for students at first but will certainly serve them well not only in the rest of this chapter but in all their academic work.

With the discussion of analogies, you might want to give your students something to practice on. One suggestion is to work again from two columns, asking students to construct an analogy by pairing something from column A with something from column B. Make sure that whatever you list in either column is complex enough to lend itself to a developed comparison. Here's an example:

A	B
public speaking	bowling
rewriting	fishing
defining	commuting
remembering	tailoring
voting	electrifying
protesting	sleeping

A Case from the History of Science (p. 222)

Encourage students to be playful with their analogies. If they see that the unexpected comparison can provide a fresh insight or a new way of looking, they may be more willing to experiment. If you'd like to stay with this process for a while, ask students to brainstorm individually and then to share their ideas in groups. The groups can then share with the whole class, or the lists can become the basis for some journal reflection.

A Case from American History (p. 223)

Jefferson and Hamilton: This is another Case which produces much better reading and discussion when students are asked to approach the passages as writers. Not much will happen unless you get students reading actively about Jefferson and Hamilton. Sometimes a good way in is to forget for awhile about the request to compare Jefferson and Hamilton, working with a single passage. A simple request like this may do the trick for the Jefferson passage: "Jefferson is regarded as one of our founding fathers but Miller does not seem to give him a lot of respect. Assemble the evidence that Miller does not think highly of Jefferson." For Hamilton: "When many people think of Alexander Hamilton, they think of money. Why?" Some such questions send students back into these texts, familarizing themselves enough that they begin to find themselves invested enough in the two descriptions to begin to function comparatively.

Students are apt to latch on too adamantly to a blank chart like the one we offer on page 224. You'll want them to use it for its heuristic value rather than to see it as a potential outline for an essay. Similarly, if students attempt to draft an essay using the subtopics we've suggested on page 233, you may find yourself with a limp set of essays. As an antidote, you might then want to work with one or more of the theses suggested on page 234. Some students may favor a clearly patterned comparison/contrast to a strongly argued one. Getting students to see that good comparisons *are* arguments will sometimes take work.

First Passes

1. Establishing Comparisons (p. 234)

You might want to read Yule's article with your students, pointing out the variety of issues he raises. The essay topics suggested with the reading can serve as a basis for informal writing or for small group work. It might be interesting, for example, to ask two small groups of students to work separately on each of the essay topics (or on any two you choose) and then to compare their results. These shorter comparisons within the larger essay may show students ways to open up a question. How are acquisition and learning different — and how are they not so different? How do the different teaching methods work? Are there connections that students can make between the two discussions?

For students in your class who have learned English as a second language, you can extend the discussion of comparison in several directions. Can they use their own experiences as language learners to comment on learning/acquisition or on any of the teaching methods? Do differences among languages come into play when the teaching methods are discussed? Which comparisons provide the most useful look at Yule's article?

This assignment offers some rich material for discussion or reflection in exploratory writing. How did they establish the comparisons? Did they reject any possibilities? How much did their own experience as language learners come into play as they worked with Yule's text (another kind of comparison)? Did the work of the separate groups differ significantly, or were there more similarities than differences? Can they speculate on why — and on how several kinds of comparing became useful?

2. Comparing Arguments (p. 239)

Although there are other ways to compare these two pieces, we've found that comparing the two writers' styles of arguing (begging the question of what we mean by "style") is a good way to keep students writing about these texts in focused ways.

By way of preliminary experiment, you might ask your students if they have any expectations about the structure of academic arguments. If asked to write an essay, pro or con, on the topic of test-tube babies, how would they expect to organize their essays? Is there a consensus among the class? What are the general expectations?

If you're successful in getting students to say much about their expectations about argumentative writing, working with these two pieces may be interesting for the ways they match and fail to match those expectations. Neither piece is a straightforward argument of the type "Here is my claim; here are some opposing views; here is my support." In fact, the assignment can help to challenge the view that there is any single prevailing style of arguing.

You may need to point out to students that neither Steinfels nor Thomas is writing against the others' argument. They haven't read each other; their sense of opposition is only toward generalized argumentative positions. We'd stress that it's not a matter of who "wins" this argument — particularly since they're not addressing each other. It's a question of looking critically at how two writers define their argumentative ground and what strategies they call upon to help them sound persuasive.

Some observations on the argumentative style of Steinfels:

Her opening paragraph sounds merely descriptive. But in what ways does the tone of the paragraph establish a climate? Which words and phrases do the job?

After paragraph 2 settles down to more description, Steinfels's attitude starts to become visible: Discussion has become "increasingly academic" and IVFs may become "just another routine." The implication is clearly that at the very least more genuinely heated debate would be a good thing.

As the sense of outrage builds, the techniques become more blunt. Ask students to identify two such techniques in paragraph 4. The two we have in mind are the use of *have* in sardonic quotes and raising the specter of lesbian motherhood.

Students may or may not be able to explain the *Brave New World* allusion. Why is this heavy artillery?

"Having loosened the biological tie." It helps, in anticipation of Thomas's argument, to ask just what is meant by this phrase. Bypassing sexual intercourse? Relocating the site of conception outside the womb? What biological ties does the procedure not loosen?

How does Steinfels arrive at the image of the day not so far off when one can "live with a minimum of human contact and human community" (p. 241)? But aren't the people attempting to have babies by extraordinary means looking for more human contact and community? How did we get to this place in Steinfels argument? What is its connection to what has come before?

What is the connotation of the term *hatcheries* and what is the justification for introducing that term?

Ask students to spell out the analogy glimpsed in the final paragraph. What seems strange and unwarranted in the words *In the same year* and *began* in the statement "But in the same year that technology brought about the birth of Elizabeth Carr, technology also began to overwhelm us with its toxic wastes, failed to build a safe nuclear power plant, and together with both nuclear and conventional weapons, seemed to bring us to the brink of war.

Does anybody recall what events in 1981 she is referring to? Even if we knew, and we agreed the events were cataclysmic, by what logic of association is Elizabeth Carr's birth ominous?

We think the kind of critical reading we solicit here can also be applied to Thomas. Although there are fewer seams to his argument, his essay can be read as a graceful effort to duck the main issue:

> Thomas's key rhetorical move is redefinition: Extra-uterine conception is not a revolutionary scientific breakthrough but "a minor technical modification." Is this a fresh analytical perspective or merely a bit of intellectual slight of hand?

> As does Steinfels, Thomas lets his tone do part of the job, with the image of the punctured paternal ego at the end of paragraph 1 and the ineffectual senate subcommittees in paragraph 2.

> Some proponents of IVF would insist that this procedure is not like hatching babies, for the fertilized egg is returned to the womb. Interestingly, Thomas, like the opponents of IVF, doesn't see any point in lingering on this distinction. Like Steinfels he is willing to foresee a point where the "technological" difficulties will be surmounted and babies brought to full term outside the womb. He allows for this possibility and insists on seeing it as no fundamental disruption.

> In Steinfels, the image of technology looms. In Thomas, technological achievements are miniaturized.

> What would Thomas make of Steinfels' fear that biological connections are somehow being loosened?

> Has anyone claimed that the genetic mysteries are not amazing? Does that mean that other biological questions with social implications aren't worth discussing? Don't new medical capabilities give rise to real social concerns? And why is "amazement" the line along which Thomas chooses to move. Is it amazement that will be setting off the senate subcommittees, or something closer to fear?

3. Comparing Poems (p. 242)

It may be helpful for students to read these poems aloud and to hear them read before they begin to work on the questions on pages 242–243. These questions might usefully serve as the basis for some class discussion followed by a short period of rough writing.

Some students may want to use the two poems to emphasize common features; but most students are far more interested in speaking about differences. And usually students want to talk about the poems in sociological ways rather than strictly literary ones, an impulse we encourage. A sociological experiment in the classroom is to ask each member of the class to write down on a slip of paper which poem he or she prefers (you also might want to add a third category, "No strong preference"). Do the stated preferences take gender lines?

When asked to account for the differences in feeling between the two poems, most students say that the difference is simple: One poem is boy-girl and the other boy-boy. "Alone with girls, boys can be tender, but put them with other boys ... " Fair enough. But this leaves us at an interpretive dead end in writing about the two poems. You'll need to convert the "because" explanations to "how" explanations. What choices, beyond the boy-girl and boy-boy starting points, enable Soto to achieve his effects?

Brainstorming a list can help:

"Oranges"	"Cruel Boys"
shorter lines	longer lines
no dialogue	dialogue
careful behavior	devil-may-care behavior
metaphorical language:	metaphors?
Tiered like bleachers	
like old coats	
fire in my hands	
eye contact	no eyes mentioned
gentle sense of touch	gritty sense of touch
images of lights	no single type of image
all seriousness	comic moments
ordered story	chaotic story
this, then this	events mixed with fantasized
held as a single memory	events
dignified details	pee-chee folders, drooped bras, walkie-talkies, spitballs
poetic experience	no interest in "poetry"
saleslady	teacher
"burned," "bright," "tiny"	"scribbled," "sludge," "scratching"

Are the "I"s of the two poems the same boy? Imagining so enables us to see a tension between two selves, in fact enables us to call in question the notion of a stable self as opposed to a situational one. Whether or not you choose to pursue the idea of a divided self, students report that it's more interesting to read these two poems together than separately.

Options

The selections in this section afford quite a range of choice. Either you may assign one or more to the entire class for writing and/or discussion, or you may allow students to make their own choices depending on their interests. You might prefer to assign one substantial piece of writing to emerge from work with one Option or several smaller essays, discussions, or journal entries ranging more freely among the selections. Whichever you choose, it's probably a good idea to remind students of the issues about comparing that their earlier work with the chapter raised. How can they establish comparisons that leave room for development? What strategies are available if their first thoughts don't prove fruitful? How do they decide which comparisons will be useful?

An Anthropology Option (p. 245)

Simply perceiving the basis of this comparison can be fun for students, who tend to be reluctant to put these texts on the same footing. At some point in the assignment, you may find it helpful to explain that some scholars have pointed out the universal nature of such stories and that earlier versions of creation stories have become, in modern times, the scientist's theories.

Once willing to look at the two texts within a common framework, as efforts to explain how things originated, students will be disposed to look for similarities. But similarities may be hard to find, and students will tend to force them. You may want to help students from the outset by letting them know that they needn't force similarities and that they want to be faithful to the great differences in the two passages. It's just that, without some framework for comparison, there's little that's interesting to contrast. If it helps, they can look at their job as *first* to discover interesting categories for comparison and *then* to show how differently the two passages work. Sometimes a chart like the following one will help:

Basis of Comparison	Text A	Text B
"In the very beginning . . ."	darkness	fireball
central character	gurra ancestor	?
?	?	temperature
Ongoing process	flowers/growth	expansion of matter
Today	The "Ilbalintja Soak"	fireball still with us

The question marks indicate places where nothing much comes quickly to mind — we think it's important to acknowledge how frequently such dead spots will occur. Still, a chart like this one can also prompt students both to discover possible bases of comparison and to identify comparable features in the two texts. By simply asking, in effect, "Is there an equivalent to this feature in Text B?" or "What's the nearest feature in B to this feature in A?" we can prompt thinking. And sometimes you may want to do some preliminary work of your own on such a chart. Plugging a feature like "flowers/growth" into a column can sometimes spark a category or comparison that would not occur to a writer without the prompt but that, once conceived, can be nicely developed.

If your students are interested in this assignment (or if you have decided to ask students to choose only one option as the basis of a more substantial piece of writing), you may want to suggest that they do a bit of research to find out more about accounts of creation. If they are working individually, you might suggest that they find an account from another culture and create a three-way comparison. Or, if they are working on these options as group projects, suggest that each bring a different account to the group and work on creating appropriate categories for comparison (thus reviewing their work from the "Classifying" chapter) and on developing essays individually or as a group. The territory is rich enough to allow for many kinds of exploration — or for working only with the original assignment.

An Education Option (p. 247)

This assignment generates plenty of writing, most of it contrastive, but very loosely so. First drafts tend to produce comments on Franklin and comments on Malcolm X, tied together only by a very general thesis and a single transition, e.g., "Unlike Franklin, Malcolm X had to learn to read as an adult." For students who do find sharp, sustained contrasts to make, Franklin tends to become a whipping boy.

There are some bases of resemblance between the two accounts, although it may take some digging to get them out: the theme of self-education, the role of debate, the motive of letter-writing, the factors of time and opportunity, even the theme of bondage. But having teased out such ideas, you'll want to be wary of making too much of them. This assignment can be an excellent vehicle for pointing out the lameness of essays of the "Here are two similarities and three differences . . . " type. Do the students' essays do justice to the sweeping rage of the Malcolm X passage, to the all-devouring political motivation of his reading, to the claim that "the ability to read awoke inside me some long dormant craving to be mentally alive"?

Despite what we've said above about the frequency with which students only loosely connect the two readings, there's much to be said for students who boldly declare "There's no real comparison here." Perceptive students sometimes point out that the Franklin with which we begin is already a reader — he is looking to do some fine-tuning and to improve his writing. Malcolm's pursuit of reading has no counterpart in Franklin since "from a child I was fond of reading" — as if he cannot remember not reading and thus recalls no time when the veil was lifted.

Passages like these two can help us pose a very real question that can be shared with our students: Does the act of comparison help us to read either passage more effectively?

The two passages also call for more context, and you might want to parcel out some research assignments, particularly for Franklin. (Franklin reappears in a later assignment in this chapter, by the way — see p. 268). Rehabilitating Franklin—and his own brand of intellectual curiosity — from the potential damage of the Malcolm X comparison might be an interesting project. Another would be to do research on Malcolm X to address the question of whether or not a comparison across such wide historical, class, and ethnic barriers would be possible, and if it is, how could one begin it?

Students who are taken with Malcolm X's account of how reading changed and shaped his life might also enjoy Richard Wright's widely anthologized essay "My Library Card." Comparing these two writers' experiences with students' own experiences of reading may provide another kind of comparison and some important insights about reading and writing.

An Art Option (p. 256)

If your students have worked with the Art Option in the "Classifying" chapter, consider returning to that assignment for a few moments to review the ways they discovered to talk about paintings. If they have not, spend a few minutes talking about the kinds of things they can say about paintings. Students who are art majors or who have taken art courses can contribute comments to get the class started. It's important for students to realize that they don't need specialized knowledge in order to tackle this assignment, however.

You might want to mention some notions for them to ponder: How can we recognize (or can we) that the two paintings were done by the same painter? What elements do they have in common? Ask students to brainstorm five or six resemblances. They may want to consider why we compare two paintings by the same artist in the first place. Are we looking for similarities, for a way of distinguishing the artist's style? Might we be looking for differences, perhaps to distinguish one period from another? Would we ask the same questions if we knew the paintings were done by different artists? Would the comparison still be useful?

Ask students to look at the artist's use of light, of human figures, and of titles. What mood is created in each painting? How does the artist create mood? If you could set the painting to music, what would you choose? Why? If you'd like to introduce background information, you could tell students that Giorgio de Chirico's art is noted for its "dream world," that at least one art historian has called him "a poetic painter" who "explains nothing" and creates a world "suspended in time." His "inexplicable cityscapes" have been described as "haunted" and his towers, smokestacks, solitary figures, and deserted squares "become fantasms, curiosities, silent and ominous" (John Canaday, *Mainstreams of Modern Art*, New York, Simon and Schuster, 1962). Or you might even ask them to do a bit of research. But you need not add anything outside the paintings. Asking them to look closely, to develop categories for their observations, and to make statements of comparison will offer sufficient opportunity for worthwhile work.

You'll probably need to argue against some students' idea that they should compare and contrast in equal degrees, to create two equal lists of like and unlike features. If they're trying to establish something about what distinguishes this artist's style, then similarities will be important. Features become more prominent when they are repeated. After they've seen the similarities, though, they may want to broaden the discussion by looking at contrasts. You can ask them, at the beginning and at the end of the conversation — or of the writing they have done — whether the similarities or the differences were more illuminating and why.

Whatever you decide to do with the discussion and the writing (we think there should be some kind of writing here, whether rough or more formal), remind students that comparing is an interpretive act, a thinking strategy, not a mechanical exercise. If they're developing a list of similarities, they have some end in mind, some idea that emerges from and unifies their search.

A Literature Option (p. 258)

As a path into these poems, you may want to give your class a bit of help with each poem individually, posing some questions for students to consider or encouraging them to come up with the questions. They could move line by line or stanza by stanza through each poem, recording observations as they go, in order to arrive at some generalizations. Sometimes, though, students are so used to writing about a poem a stanza at a time that they forget that they're seeking some general meaning. You may need to remind them.

With Emily Dickinson's poem, you might use sequencing as a way to raise some questions, noting confusions and marking shifts in time. Mermaids in the basement? Frigates with hands? A mouse aground? Why "no Man moved Me"? Such observations might encourage students to establish initially how strange a poem this seems to be and to read it attentively, not trying to figure it out prematurely.

Another sequential strategy is to ask students to look for the "real" divisions of the poem, moments when something seems to be changing. In fact, you might ask students to choose a sequence of such moments, asking them to characterize the shift with a strong verb: Here the mood darkens, here the Tide swells, here something intensifies, here something ebbs. Then ask students to describe the movement of the poem in a simple series of phases, calling attention to the places where important shifts seem to occur. Not everyone will agree upon where those shifts occur, but it's probably important if class discussion arrives at some consensus about a few points. For example, we all can agree that whereas the second stanza continues in the vein of the first, the "But" of the third stanza brings an abrupt shift as Mr. Tide arrives.

Hogan's poem may at first be seen as a series of exchanges: "He said, then I said, then he said, then I said . . . . " Ask students how they would characterize the pattern of these exchanges. Do they see movement — toward seduction, for example? Or toward something else?

Another way to sequence the poem is as a series of surprises. Much will depend, of course, on what students choose to define as surprises, and you might also want to try classifying the surprises (mild, shocking, comic?). One bumpy tour through the poem, for instance, might highlight this sequence:

He wore a suede jacket.	(line 3)
— all bones	(line 9)
You can tell the bones nothing, sí?	(line 13)
He put his hand inside my dress.	(line 17)
I am a taxpayer,	(line 18)
Will you have some guacamole?	(line 28)
You don't make good corners	(line 30)
Señorita, I will call you up	(line 34)
They think with their genitals	(line 40)
and held him a little tighter.	(line 43)

This might be a good moment to break off the discussion and ask students to write about the two poems comparatively. They can choose a focus that allows them to explore what they observe in reading each: themes, tone of voice, language, speaker, title. They may want to write about how each is about more than it seems at the start (why "Etc." in Hogan's title, for example). Caution students to stay with each poem instead of moving away from the texts, using specific lines and images to support their interpretations. After they have written their interpretations, you might ask students to reflect on the juxtaposition of the two poems. Did reading the two together make students more likely to read themes of sex and death into Dickinson's poem, for example?

Again, students should note that serializing and comparing can work together as interpretive strategies and that both are powerful tools for interpretation, not simply forms to be filled in.

A Political Science Option (p. 260)

These readings by Nkrumah and Fieldhouse ask to be read and reread. Understanding often shifts or enlarges on second or third reading, a fact that some students are somewhat reluctant to acknowledge or act on. In this assignment, as in many that students will encounter elsewhere, rereading is essential to both understanding and successful writing.

The readings don't lend themselves to an informed discussion of African politics or economics, but they do lend themselves to a contrast of rhetorics. Both passages are ideologically loaded. Nkrumah's perspective is decidedly from the left and that of a political participant; Fieldhouse's is vaguely from the right and that of a professional outsider, an academic. But for students both passages may seem cast in impenetrable academese. All the more reason for trying to distinguish between the two brands of jargon.

One strategy to get students started is to have them list for each writer either all the words they don't understand or all the words they find characteristic of one writer but not the other. Here is one student's combined list, terms she felt she didn't understand but which seemed characteristic of the writer:

Nkrumah	**Fieldhouse**
paradox	ideological concepts
neo-colonialism	semantics
impoverishment	pejorative
primary ores	unrequited advantage
arable	variable capital
imperialist exploitation	neo-Marxist terminology
productive methods	imperialist superprofit
imperialist exploiters	metropolitan policy
lush verbiage	tariffs
	entrepreneurs
	stimulus of overseas markets
	mise en valeur
	extractive industries
	patterns of colonial economy
	commercial metrocentrism
	uneven development
	perspective view
	alien rule
	substantive

Another way to begin is with some questions like these: Do Nkrumah and Fieldhouse agree on any facts? Do they employ any common terminology? Do they identify any similar problems?

One way into a comparison is through the "problem of exploitation." For Nkrumah exploitation is a problem because it occurs: The problem is that Africa has been exploited by Europeans. For Fieldhouse exploitation is a problem because it's a difficult term to define, and he spends several paragraphs dancing around the two definitions, "use" and "superprofit," comfortable with the first and skeptical of the second.

Stylistically, Nkrumah's method is one of assumption and assertion. Fieldhouse's is one of pompous hesitation and qualification. His characteristic claim is that data are insufficient: the economic development of Africa is "too vast a subject to be comprehended," present research materials provide "an insufficient basis," "very little is known" about the activities of merchants, "sophisticated data on production does not exist." These sort of demurrals do, of course, amount to a claim — that anyone else who attempts to describe what occurred hasn't looked for the facts, or they would know how murky they are. But what, then, does Fieldhouse believe? We arrive at something in the final paragraph, although still abundantly qualified: On the whole, although it could have been done more compassionately, European development brought Africa "forcibly into the world economy." Much labor for little fruit.

For Nkrumah "development" is passing Africa by. The gap between European and African development has widened over time. There are enormous resources for development in Africa, but control of this development still belongs to Western countries. For Fieldhouse African development seems to be progressing.

Selective reading of Fieldhouse can produce statements quite compatible with the perspective of Nkrumah. On page 263, for example, Fieldhouse describes more specifically than Nkrumah the nature of postcolonial exploitation: "By the 1950s much of French Africa was so tied to France by high price levels and dependence on a protected market that independence brought little freedom to choose future economic policy."

If with this assignment you find your class floundering but curious (as opposed to floundering and listless), we'd suggest building in a research component. Ask each student to research a different African country and prepare a three- or four-minute report for the next class. A perfectly adequate source is the *World Almanac*, which gives thumbnail descriptions of the history, language, political climate, and economic health of each country. The general issue to have each report address: How has the country been affected by its relation to the West? The exercise may lead you away from the Nkrumah/Fieldhouse comparision but toward some clarification of the issues they address.

A History Option (p. 264)

Students who have considered some of the assignments in the "Summarizing" chapter will be familiar with the notion that different writers select different materials according to their purpose and perspective. If students have done the Political Science Option on stages of a political event (p. 260) in "Serializing," they have already considered how news media select different details to reveal different perspectives on events. In their work with the other assignments in this chapter, too, students have seen how to select a framework for comparison that highlights some information and makes other information less important or even irrelevant. Therefore, it should not surprise them that an American and a British historian will have different perspectives on the American Revolution and will choose to tell the story differently.

The Trevelyan piece makes for some surprises, since from his perspective the Revolution is seen not in heroic terms but as a series of diplomatic and political blunders by the English government. From his perspective the American Revolution has had "consequences that we rue to this day" — a fresh perspective, for most students.

Before looking at either of these pieces, you might ask students, singly or in groups, to write their own short chronology of the American Revolution. It may be interesting for the class as a whole to compare their versions. Such an exercise, incidentally, should prepare students to see that Morgan's own treatment, which is certainly a more familiar version than Trevelyan's, is itself a quite selective interpretation of events.

You'll also want to acknowledge that while these two perspectives are quite different, there is nevertheless also a strong chord of agreement running through the two accounts. For instance, both emphasize British mismanagement, the size and inertia of the loyalists, the crucial and not altogether foresighted role of the French, and the pivotal role of Saratoga. In fact, some students may find the two accounts similar enough that it may take a while to get them to see differences in perspective that seem to us quite sharp.

For an interesting companion piece to this assignment, you might want to look at a column of Sydney Harris appearing in his collection of columns *Strictly Personal* (1977). "One Person's Facts Are Another's Fiction" illustrates how differently a short description of John Hancock can read from opposed historical perspectives, one American, one British.

For a short spin-off assignment, ask students to choose an event or person they're familiar with and to select different facts or details to present this event or person from two different perspectives. The related acts of imagining and selecting can be fun to write and fun to share with the whole class.

Reflecting on Comparison

Most students come to our classes with some experience in writing an essay labeled "compare and contrast." They are familiar with patterns for this essay: all A then all B, or one feature A, one feature B, and so on. What may well be new to them in this chapter is to consider comparing as a strategy for interpretation rather than as a form to be filled in with appropriate details. This may be the first time they think about comparing as governed by a purpose (other than to fulfill the demands of a specific assignment) or about ways to develop both a helpful overall focus and useful points of comparison. You might ask students to reflect briefly in their journals about differences between their past work with comparing and ways they've been asked to use the strategy now. Or ask about the similarities.

Many instructors report that essay exams that include comparison questions present a particular problem. Students use the question as an opportunity to write everything they know, to recite facts, or to identify terms, in the hope of somehow including "what the teacher wanted" rather than to establish and develop points of comparison. You may want to spend a few minutes discussing this kind of exam question with students and helping them to see how their work with this chapter has enabled them to approach such questions effectively.

You might want to ask students to think about contexts for comparing, about the kinds of situations, tasks, and questions that might call for a comparative strategy. Consider returning to one or more of the "Classifying" assignments:

> The opening problem on metaphors for the writing process: Can they see useful comparisons among the categories they created?
>
> The Anthropology Option on body language among college students: If they observed in a different kind of location, what differences and similarities would they notice?
>
> The Economics Option: What do they now see as the comparative strengths and weaknesses of these perspectives?
>
> The Literature Option with openings of nonfiction passages: Can they compare language, expectations, approach to the reader among the categories they created for grouping these or among several individual passages?

Of course you won't want to return to all of these problems, and you may prefer to return to other assignments instead. But it's not a bad idea, if time and your plan for the class permit, to allow students an opportunity to look again at earlier work and to think about ways to combine strategies to expand their interpretive choices.

Chapter 6

Analyzing (p. 274)

On page 276 we try to articulate the definition of analysis underlying this chapter. By insisting that analytical writing is never merely a matter of looking closely at component parts but of looking from a particular perspective or framework, we hope to keep students critically alert to the shaping power of such frameworks. Our method through most of the chapter is to offer students something to analyze and one or more vantage points from which to analyze it. The danger in this method, we know, is that students may latch on to the mechanism uncritically: They may look to the framing text for a ready-made thesis to slap on the text to be analyzed. For this reason, we urge you to cultivate some skepticism toward the framing texts.

Working with the Strategy

After your students have read the interview and the perspective, you may want to engage them in a brief discussion of Jung's argument, examining the meaning of "mythic" man and "scientific" man. Why does Jung feel that "the mythic side" of humanity is "given short shrift nowadays"? You'll want to keep this brief, but it may be helpful for students to articulate and share their understandings as they work with the text.

Students may be able to see quite a string of inventions in the child's descriptions, some even qualifying as "glamour" in Jung's sense: the resurrection after four days, the angels, wings, brightness and cleanliness, cake, clouds, play.

And some students may not see a good fit between Jung's theory and the interview. They may wonder about some of the details that don't seem to fit together: "It's bad to go to heaven because you have to fly" set next to the fun of being able to fly and play hide and seek. Or they may comment on the gender specialization of the tasks in heaven. Some may see the vision of a stove for every angel as anything but glamorous! These dissatisfactions are worth encouraging, as we'll be asking students to think about both the value and the limitations of using a perspective throughout the chapter.

Cases

A Case from Psychology (p. 277)

In this Case, we offer an extended example that should help illustrate both the power and the limitations of a framing perspective. The excerpt from John

Fowles's *The Collector* looks very different at first sight from the perspective offered by the framing idea of "the Stockholm syndrome"; and it looks different still when students are invited out from under the influence of that idea. For maximum illustrative power, you might want to treat this example as an in-class exercise. Before asking students to read over the chapter introduction, try giving them a photocopy of the passage from *The Collector* and then proceed in the four stages we describe. Having worked through analyses of their own, students should be more receptive to following our discussion — perhaps more ready to pull away from the Stockholm syndrome as an altogether satisfactory explanation.

The student essays point up both the benefits and the frustrations of working with the perspective. Students need to notice the differences in interpretation and the ways the writers develop their positions and to think about what it means to use a perspective — not to adopt it without question or challenge but to explore its usefulness in thinking analytically.

Cases from Biology and Literature (p. 282)

The Case from Biology asks students to interpret the data in a table, a familiar task if they have worked with the tables in earlier chapters. This kind of assignment asks them to look closely and not just to describe but to find some meaning in what they see.

Incidentally, the student analysis on pages 285–286 is somewhat controversial. Not all biology teachers would find it equally welcome: Some maintain that the speculative questions raised by the student writer are a bit naive and a bit distracting — in short, unprofessional (if the experimental data are so suspicious, the experiment must not have been well conceived in the first place); others see both the substance and the tone as entirely appropriate to a student report.

The assignment that accompanies the Rich poem should sound familiar; it's probably the most frequently given kind of analytic assignment. The discussion that follows presents ways to approach the task, including an example of how to find and consider lines of inquiry, rejecting unfruitful ones. This brief depiction of a writer running into dead ends may be worth emphasizing; some students are in the habit of latching onto the first idea that comes to mind without considering other possibilities.

We've deliberately left the analysis of the Rich poem undeveloped. You may want your students to take up the invitation we extend on page 290. Diverse students have found diverse things to say about this poem. If you're stuck for an angle of approach, you might suggest that we read the poem as a meditation on a marriage, or marriage in general. But that's the sort of frame — like the Stockholm idea — that can forestall other insights. It's better to let people work on their own for a time and see what emerges.

Comparing their interpretations after they have worked on them should open up a range of possibilities.

A Case from a History Exam (p. 291)

Our last analytical Case also lends itself to classroom experiment. Ask students to freewrite a draft or sketch an outline in response to the foreign policy question. See what sort of responses you get. We've encountered a remarkable variety —

from those which show students unsure what the phrase *foreign policy* means to those which make persuasive decade-by-decade distinctions.

First Passes

1. Applying a Perspective (p. 291)

Much of the difficulty of this assignment lies with the initial reading, "The Moral Basis of Literacy Instruction." We suggest asking students first to paraphrase or summarize the two paragraphs from Graff. We've noticed that the first paragraph can be difficult, partly because it identifies "literacy" (rather than schooling) as its topic and because it's cast in the passive voice. From what point of view is the paragraph proceeding? It's hard to follow. But the start of the second paragraph helps us to read the first one: The phrase "these moral functions of schooling" helps us to see that the first paragraph is about the moral functions of schooling (but it may not help us to see, yet, that *moral* is in Graff's usage a socially loaded term, equivalent to *manipulative*). Only after reading the paragraphs several times, preferably with the help of some class discussion, are students apt to emerge with an accurate paraphrase such as "According to Graff, widespread schooling helped to teach workers to be punctual, efficient, and undisruptive; more important it taught them not to aspire to other kinds of lives." In other words, in our experience, it takes considerable time and effort to arrive at an understanding that Graff is saying something iconoclastic about education. Sometimes student paraphrases will even successfully mask their failing to make that fundamental discovery about the text.

In our experience, too, many students will be unfamiliar with the term *alienation*. And even after explaining the term to one another they will be unprepared for Graff's implication that a state of alienation can be seen as something positive, something that less manipulative educations *achieve*.

Only after students have wrestled with the Graff will they be ready to analyze the literacy lessons from his point of view. Without that perspective students may be quick to see the lessons as silly, but seldom as anything more than harmlessly silly. Armed with the Graff, the lessons light up propagandistically: Writers not only note the italicized *"You must not vaunt or boast your skill"* but find the "ominous" moral overtones in sentences like "Pause at the stops or points" (do what you're told) and "It is fraud to take what is not yours" (hands off the company property). Viewed from this aggressive perspective, there's even something entrancingly defensive about the sentence "It is not my fault, if you do not learn to read." But of course from Graff's point of view it's not merely the moral content of the sentences that's noteworthy; it's also their discontinuity (Don't try to make any sense of this, but here are some words and here's how you should pronounce them).

Some of the best discussions of these texts occur when students are moved to defend the lessons, or to claim that to come at them from Graff's perspective is to overread them. One wonderful argument contended that in Lesson XXI the repetition of the "au" sound, together with the entertainingly absurd lack of connections among sentences, is utterly at odds with any tacit effort by the educational system to "get these kids in line." The tone, whether deliberate or not, is one of anarchic playfulness. And one student had great fun rewriting the lesson from a "Graffian educational point of view": "Why is wine kept in vaults? I cannot laud the cause. Let's pause to see the fraud . . . ."

The second lesson is more explicit in its moral instruction. Students are likely to comment on the lessons within the penmanship exercise: "Avoid rudeness of manner. Be always ready to do good. Correct some fault in every line." How do these seemingly innocuous bits of instruction in upright behavior fit with Graff's ideas about schooling?

If your students have worked with the first example in the "Comparing" chapter, you might want to make a connection to expand the analytic perspective here. Do they see parallels between the views of workers discussed in those two excerpts and Graff's comments on the purposes of education? How does our understanding of people and their role in society (or in the workplace) influence what they are taught and how they are "managed"? In answering questions like these, students can see firsthand how the application of a perspective can influence behavior and not just academic understanding.

2. Evaluating a Perspective (p. 294)

This assignment might be used loosely in conjunction with the Stockholm syndrome exercise that we walk through on pages 277–282. In both cases, psychologists propose explanations of considerable explanatory power for behavior during hostage-takings; yet both cases also support some healthy skepticism toward the psychologists' theories.

In analyzing "Gunman" from the point of view offered by Seligman, students will want to stress any evidence they can find for Rose's reasons to feel helpless (are there any besides his multiple sclerosis?), his frenetic behavior during the incident, and the testimony from his mother that he had felt "depressed." They may also want to stress what Rose does to express a sense of control — finding the girl, ordering her to undress, making demands to the police, threatening to use a weapon. To make the "helpless" analysis hold up, writers will probably want to emphasize how the recent medical diagnosis must have imposed itself on the long-term depression with which Rose had evidently lived for some time.

Students who resist the "helplessness" application point out that we have too little information from which to draw conclusions. The account by Wallace and Waters is a news story compiled at some distance from the event, based evidently on police reports and an interview with Rose's mother. Seligman's "drive for competence" may seem a plausible explanation, but it doesn't rule out others. Rose certainly seems to have been "depressed," but can we be confident that Seligman's perspective enables us to understand what made this particular depressed person behave violently?

If your students seem to need a bit more practice in working with and looking critically at a perspective, try casting this assignment in the form of dialogue or an exchange of letters. Ask them first to speak or write as if they were Seligman analyzing Rose's behavior. Then suggest that they speak or write as a second person, bringing in the "yes, but" arguments. If you're working on the material in class — a good strategy here — you might even ask students to engage in debate and then to make some notes about which voice they find more convincing and why. Or they can debate about the limitations and strengths of both in explaining Rose's behavior. No matter what they decide, students are likely to benefit from reading Seligman closely and from using that close reading as a lens through which to examine Rose's behavior.

3. Evaluating Multiple Perspectives (p. 297)

This assignment is typical of the kinds of work students will be asked to do in some classes, so sorting through the data and the perspectives is a useful exercise. You may want them to work in pairs or small groups initially, looking at the graphics one at a time in light of each perspective, then comparing notes before they move on to expand the viewing field.

We recommend that you begin the assignment by asking students first to play around a bit with the tables and the chart. But of course there's nothing to prevent students familiar with the rhythm of the text from looking ahead to the theoretical passages. To begin with the theoretical passages, ask students to specify their differences of orientation and approach.

Figure 1 seems to tell the simplest story, so you might find it the best place to begin discussion. The U.S. shift in this century toward a fattier diet is presumably a dangerous trend and can be related, according to Mayer, to an increase in coronary disease. But the chart itself tells only part of the dietary story. In fact, the carbohydrate portion of the pie-chart is deceptive, Brody suggests, for there are important distinctions to be made between kinds of carbohydrates. A research question: The chart is based on 1976 figures. Since the 1980s there has been much publicity in favor of decreasing the fat content of our diets. What are the latest figures of the USDA? Where would students go to find out?

The table "What's in Fast Foods?" lends itself to several sorts of generalizations. It can be used to argue, variously, that fast foods do a good job in providing nutrition, that they contribute to caloric overload, and that they evidence our society's increasingly fatty diet. But that last generalization is a glib one. The chart certainly does not support the perception that fast foods are in some way leading or exaggerating the trend to fats over carbohydrates: A meal of Big Macs, for example, would only correspond to the national proportions for all consumption. In fact, when students actually start to do some calculations, surprising conclusions start to emerge. For example, fast foods in general seem to be doing a superlative job of delivering protein. And pizza — even pepperoni pizza! — provides not only a proportion of protein but a more favorable carbohydrate-to-fat ratio than the national averages for 1909–1913. "What 'kinds' of carbohydrates are in pizza?" students start to ask. And if you're lucky enough to find the curiosity level rising as the class goes on, students will start to raise other questions that you (and we) can't answer.

Ask the class to evaluate the perspectives and the tables in light of their own experience and what they observe around them. In fact, if you'd like to spend a bit more time here, suggest a short ethnographic study: Interview customers at fast food restaurants about their eating habits and the degree to which they're influenced by nutritional charts posted there. If you can find people who do *not* eat fast food, ask how they decide what to eat, whether they ever eat in restaurants, and how aware they are of the nutritional content of their food. How do these observations of actual behavior, combined with people's accounts of their own behavior, fit with the perspectives offered in this assignment?

And when students reflect on their experience of shifting perspectives, ask them also to think about whether anything is missing. Can they imagine a third perspective that might be helpful here? Are there other sorts of facts that might be helpful to a more complete analysis? Do they have any questions that are left unanswered? Are important issues not addressed?

Options

A Sociology Option (p. 301)

The perspective and the real-life experiences that constitute this assignment offer students an opportunity to think both about how a theory helps us understand and also how actual situations rarely fit perfectly with any theory. They may look at how the theory illuminates the experiences, enabling us to see commonalities we might otherwise miss. At the same time, they'll want to think about how the accounts don't fit within the perspective, perhaps offering alternative explanations which link the immigrant experiences presented here.

This assignment lends itself to personal essays as well as to the analysis of texts. Many students, not only recent immigrants but anyone who has experienced a sudden shift in environment, will find themselves with vivid experiences ready at hand. The power of those experiences should drive the essays that students choose to write — the theory of culture shock described by Brink and Saunders may serve merely as a pretext for that writing. Nevertheless, at some point along the way, you may want to remind students of the assignment's analytical orientation: Do their own experiences support Brink and Saunders's way of looking at culture shock, or does the four-stage representation fail to get at the heart of the experience?

Those who do work analytically with the texts will want to examine the three immigrant narratives in relation to the four-phase model described by Brink and Saunders. That model can be used to get a handle on at least two of the three narratives; on the other hand, each of them relates somewhat problematically to that model, and none shows an immigrant going through all four phases sequentially.

Although Mary Antin begins her account by looking with detachment at the context of her arrival in the United States, she quickly abandons that detachment to take us back into the experience itself. While we are conscious as we read of the older woman who is doing the recounting, the experience described is that of the unadulterated "honeymoon." When students categorize her narrative this way they often also point out that Antin's narrative can't be used to support the four-phase explanation, since her story stops at phase 1. And her tone does little to indicate whether or not she experienced frustrations later.

Maxine Hong Kingston's account of her Chinese-American childhood is problematic in many ways. Hers does not seem a classic case of culture shock in that she doesn't remember a time when she was not in the United States. Nor is there any evidence that she ever went through a honeymoon period. And to call her early experiences with U.S. schools a phase of "disenchantment" is to imply that they were preceded by a time more pleasing. So, too, it's forcing things to identify these early school years with the "Beginning Resolution Phase," even if we can detect some small resolutions going on. Yet if ever there seemed to be a case of culture shock, Kingston's is it. Does her narrative force us to question the adequacy of Brink and Saunders's definition? Or does it prompt us to consider Kingston's as a special case? We might argue that to experience culture shock in the classic sense one must move from one culture to another: Kingston's childhood dilemma may be that she is never securely in or out of Chinese culture.

Is Wood Chuen Kwong in the honeymoon phase, the disenchantment phase, the "Beginning Resolution Phase," or the "Effective Function Phase"? One effective way to structure class discussion is to ask students to make the best case they can for each phase. By selectively treating the evidence, students have made at least momentarily plausible cases for all four — with only the honeymoon phase being shouted down quickly. In most discussions of any length, the disenchantment phase gets discounted too. Kwong has found plenty in American culture to be disenchanted with, but despite the complaints, he has pretty clearly come to terms with his situation. Still, the testimony is rich enough to keep students arguing back and forth for some time.

The best essays to emerge from this assignment usually come to regard the four-phase description of culture shock as something useful but hardly ironclad. It's a useful exercise for demonstrating that idealized patterns seldom correspond neatly to case-by-case experience.

If you'd like to spend a bit more time with this assignment, there are several possibilities. Ask students to look at their own, their parents', or grandparents' experiences of coming to America in light of the perspective. Or have them return to the immigration assignment in the "Summarizing" chapter: Ask how this perspective and these personal accounts broaden their view of the earlier data. If you have saved those sections to use here, you may want to ask students to look at all the materials together to see what generalizations emerge. That exercise will probably work best with small groups of students who can then compare notes, perhaps in preparation for a longer paper. Or you might ask specific questions. How do the personal accounts illuminate the tables, or vice versa? How does the chronology look if viewed through the lens of this perspective?

A Sociology Option (p. 313)

Punk rock is already passé, but it still serves as a vehicle for trying out psychological and sociological generalizations. Although you may not want to risk the tedium of having students work out separate analyses of the punk rock scene from five points of view, we do think that the value of this assignment lies in getting students to detect and express differences of approach and emphasis among the theorists. Questions like "How might Laing's understanding of punk rock behavior differ from that of Lorenz?" are worth asking. One way to get students engaged in making such distinctions is to work in groups, making one group responsible for a Freudian interpretation, and so on. The limitation in doing this, however, is that each group's interpretation can start a sound very similar unless honed against another with which the group disagrees.

An alternative approach is to ignore the punk rock passage for a while. Ask students to paraphrase and compare the theoretical passages. Or they might try to clarify these passages along a continuum. Here, for example, is one person's sketch of how each theorist might explain aggressive behavior.

Freud: Aggression as instinctual endowment, lying in wait, looking
for provocations.

Dollard: Aggression is a feature of adolescence and is directed
toward the substitutes for one's real goals.

Reisman: It's not aggressive behavior for natural or instinctive
reasons but for peer approval. Adolescents especially are "other-
directed," shaping behavior, in this case aggression, so as to
win the approval of others.

Lorenz: Aggression is a natural response to crowding but can find
few permissible channels in modern society.

Laing: Aggression, like other destructive behavior, is a response to
the alienating conditions of our experience in the world.

And here's an attempt to group these views:

For Freud and Lorenz, aggression is part of a human's instinctual
equipment but always at odds with civilized behavior. For Dollard
and Reisman, aggression is just one of the forms that social
behavior takes; it's not in conflict with social norms — it is a
social norm. For Laing aggression is also seen as normal, but in a
society that has become absurd. For Freud and Lorenz, society is
always suppressing aggression; for Laing society expresses aggression.

After having students work out some such interpretation of the interpreters,
send students back to the punk rock essay. At this point, you might want to
simplify their job by asking them to restrict themselves to examining two
perspectives that they find in sharp disagreement. How would Freud and Reisman
analyze the events described in the punk rock article? Which approach seems
more compatible with what we know about the situation?

In the interests of skepticism, you may also want students to think about
the medium that brings us information about punk rock. Can we presume that
Goldstein's report is full and accurate, or might it be skewed in some way? Does
he himself write about the punk rock scene from a special perspective, and is
that perspective more compatible with some theories than with others?

A Science Option (p. 319)

Keller's perspective and the account of biologist Anna Brito's experience raise
a variety of issues for students to consider. Before they read about Brito, you
may want to talk with them about the issues Keller raises. What pattern does
she see in scientific discovery? How does language figure into the scientist's
ability or inability to communicate what he or she sees or, in fact, to the ability
to see what someone else claims to have discovered? Ask students what *extralogical*
and *extrarational* mean and how these terms help us understand the communication difficulties Keller describes. You may also want to explore with them
the idea that the language or the perspective shapes what we can see — in science
and in other fields as well.

When students write about Brito's story, in a formal paper or in a more
exploratory journal entry, they'll want to think about what stood in the way of
her communicating her discovery. To what extent does Keller's "lens" provide
a useful insight into Brito's experience? What were the "realm of common

experience" and the "common language" that Brito did not share? Her pathology background needed to be translated into experimental terms — because those around her worked within an experimental framework, they could not see her results as valid until she could confirm them with the kinds of data they recognized. How, then, is common language an issue for Brito?

Students may also want to raise issues not directly addressed in Keller's perspective. How, for example, do cultural misunderstanding and misreading figure into Brito's inability to have her findings recognized? Brito describes herself as a "little Portuguese woman." Is she pointing to an underlying racism or antifemale sentiment in the lab? Are there feminist issues here, particularly in terms of patterns of assertiveness and respect? If students have worked with the "Classifying" chapter, they might want to think about the ways Brito was categorized by those around her. Which labels did they apply and what were the effects of those labels?

If your class has worked with the First Passes in the "Summarizing" chapter, they might want to make connections with "Summarizing an Argument" on viruses. Keller's theory may be applied to that selection as well as to Brito's experience. What conclusions can they draw from expanding the field this way?

If you're interested in pointing some students toward Keller's book on Barbara McClintock they'll be able to examine these issues in more detail. McClintock was unable to communicate her scientific findings because of the kind of communication breakdown Keller describes: She did not say what others expected to hear and so they were unable to hear, understand, and accept her findings. If some of your students would like to use the book as the basis for a longer piece of writing, they will learn how communication can get in the way of scientific discovery and how language and custom create a filter through which we are able to see some things and not others.

A Political Science Option (p. 327)

This assignment departs from the rhythm of text and frame. The three models of political decision making are presented without a case to exercise on, and, moreover, they are presented by a single commentator — Graham Allison. But the theoretical issues are engaging enough to sustain the class interest. In fact, an account of a specific political crisis and its attendant decisions might obscure the issues, since it's Allison's contention that most commentators tacitly assume the "rational policy model" in presenting their accounts.

You might want to settle in this Option for student essays that simply help to clarify, via thoughtful paraphrase, the theoretical issues. It's quite an accomplishment just to explain the "Organizational Process Model," with its specialized terminology ("sensors," "routines," "outputs," "programs," — largely the language of computer programming), and then to differentiate it from the "Bureaucratic Politics Model," with its bargaining language. To imagine a government's crucial decisions shaped as much by political infighting as by external necessities in an arresting perspective but difficult to grasp and, once grasped, difficult to maintain.

You might want to ask students whether Allison's presentation of the three models is a dispassionate one or whether he has a point of view of his own to advance. Students will often say he does not. So it's worth discussing his argument: He seems to be arguing against the naive application of the rational model and in favor of the recognition of the other two; or we could say that he thinks we ought to be able to keep all three models in mind as we seek to understand particular decisions.

For Allison's own account of how the Cuban missile decisions can be analyzed from the three points of view he sketches, see his article in *The American Political Science Review* (September 1969). Also see his subsequent books — Allison's work on the Cuban missile crisis has become something of an academic industry. There are two features that make recent research of the missile crisis even richer than what Allison had to work with: (1) Much material that was originally classified has now become public, and (2) testimony now exists from the Russian side, so that it's possible to examine how both sets of decisions were reached.

Allison's three models are offered explicitly as ways of analyzing decisions of foreign policy. You might ask students whether they think the same three models can be applied to important federal decisions of domestic policy. Ask them to write about a domestic issue that has been in the newpapers recently. How might a proponent of the three models try to apply them?

Or ask students to invent a corporation with competing departments, each trying to convince top management to see an issue in a way most beneficial to itself. Imagine a conversation or a series of memos intended to shape a decision. How would management respond and why? Or describe a school or a family in a similar way. Your students' inventiveness in deciding what to examine can make the assignment fun at the same time as it gives them a chance to work with the three models.

You may also want to discuss with your students the questions the models raise. How, for example, does information reach decision-makers? Purveyors of information often espouse a certain view or course of action because it makes them look good or puts them in the forefront of the action, for example. The questions of how people get information, who provides it, and how it is shaped are central to our understanding that what we think and what "they" (any they) want us to think may not be in synch with what "is." (If, indeed, there's any way to determine what is!)

A thought: If you're at a point in your course where a break from routine seems necessary or appropriate, try showing the movie *Dr. Strangelove* as the "text" to examine through Allison's perspective.

A Literature Option (p. 330)

In this assignment, too, we step away from the text and perspective format; here the perspective is implicit. Students will need to read and think about the Chandler chapter and about the detective stories they have read or viewed in movies or on television before they talk about the traditions of standard detective fare. If students will be developing a longer paper from this assignment, you might suggest that they also watch one or two old detective movies or that they read some detective stories.

Prucha's imitation is deliberate, and her slant gives the story and the tradition a new angle. Students may think about the ways in which books (movies, music, and so on) speak to us through other books (movies, music, and so on) and how the echoes of Chandler ring through Prucha's story. At the same time they'll want to consider the differences. They may write about the humor of the way the Prucha story uses the stereotype — and of the stereotype itself. Neither simple satire nor just parody, "Murder Is My Business" sounds familiar precisely because it works within a genre familiar through books, movies, TV shows — and yet none of those familiar sources has a lesbian detective. As an experiment, you might have students read the last scene of Prucha's story first and then ask them to talk or write about what's going on. Do they assume the narrator is male? Why? Ask them to write (rough journal entries are appropriate) about the scene again after they have read the entire story. How do they respond? The initial thinking and discussing, combined with some exploratory writing, should give students enough to go on for a longer paper, if you've assigned one. Or you may prefer just to talk with them about how they see the Prucha story through the lens of the Chandler chapter. Would they see it differently without the perspective? Are there features they wouldn't notice if they read only the one story without considering the other?

A Literature Option (p. 345)

As the final Option in this chapter, we've given students an analytic assignment that resembles many they'll see in academic settings. Unlike the Allison Option, which provides only frames, or the Chandler-Prucha, which sets texts next to each other and asks students to develop the perspective, this one provides only one text, Reginald McKnight's "The Kind of Light That Shines on Texas." Within any course, students would read this story in the context of the semester's ongoing discussions of literature. Even within that context, though, students will need to develop a question or a perspective that provides something interesting to look at. We hope that by having attempted other assignments in this chapter and elsewhere in the book, students will have developed an understanding of the need not just for a thesis but for an informing perspective.

You might want to begin by asking students to jot down their responses during and after an initial reading of the story. They could then compare notes in small group and/or whole class discussion and list the ideas and issues that emerge. Another possible strategy would involve asking students to complete this sentence "This is a story about . . . " in as many ways as they can, with the restriction that they may not simply summarize plot. These lists should point up many of the story's themes. To lead students a step further toward formulating an argument, you might ask them to take the list to a second stage: "This is not so much a story about . . . as about . . ." Sharing these lists in class should provide a variety of writing possibilities for students to consider.

Or you might want to try a traditional question — "Discuss the light imagery in the story," for example — and show students how to use the thinking strategies they've worked with so far to tackle the question. They could, for example, look at definitions of "light" along with connotations of the word and what it means in context each time it's used in the text and in the title. They could try summarizing the story with an eye toward finding meaning in the uses of light and dark (as they may have done with language in "English as a Second Language" if you have worked with that story). They could look at images of light and dark in sequence and see if an interesting pattern emerges. Of course, they could list all the references to light and try classifying, finding categories that give them a way to look at the story. They might think about the title, as well as about what, if anything, is illuminated in the story. Do they, for example, see the ending as confirming or rejecting the platitudes that one might expect to emerge from this sort of story — about growing up, racism, relationships between generations, learning the harsh truths of the world? Is it less than crystal clear what the narrator learns? The objective is to find something interesting to write about, to find a perspective from which to interpret the story instead of just providing a list of observations.

Reflecting on Analyzing

Analyze. This may well be the instruction students will see most often in their academic careers. In this chapter, we've tried to give students some ways to think about the word and the thinking processes it entails. You may want to ask your students to think about some of the questions we've raised. How does the perspective, the lens through which you look define and shape — and limit — what you can see? How can you develop a perspective when none is provided? How can the other strategies with which you've worked so far help you define a perspective from which to analyze a text or an idea?

Many of the assignments in the chapter ask students to do two things simultaneously: to look through a particular perspective at a text or a set of data and then to look critically at the perspective itself — to look both through and at the lens. Ask students to think about why each way of looking is useful to them; what can they learn by bringing one idea to bear upon another, and why is it important to examine the lens as well? This double operation should be valuable to students as they approach work in other classes, or even as they read the newspaper or watch the TV news. If you want to spend a bit more time here, ask them to read a newspaper — front page, editorial section, or feature article — and to try to identify the perspective through which any one writer looks at a news event. How does the perspective shape what is reported? Are there times when they would need to know more about the perspective to be able to look at it critically? How might it be problematic for their understanding of an event to be shaped by a perspective they aren't really aware of? They could, in connection with this assignment, look back at their work in "Serializing" on interpreting a news event sequentially. How is selection shaped by the lens through which a writer views an event? This might be a good time to look again at the Tompkins piece in "Serializing"; if you have not worked with the piece, you might want to introduce it in connection with this chapter. At the same time as she traces her own intellectual journey, Tompkins looks at various ways of seeing Indians and the effects each perspective has on what is seen.

As a final reflection on this chapter and those that preceded it, you might consider with your students that the purpose of using and examining different strategies is not to collect inventory — any more than a list is the same as serializing or a simple recounting of events is the same as summarizing. They need to be aware of the strategies they're using, to be able to make fruitful choices, to be able to test ways of thinking to find those that are most useful for arriving at interpretations of texts of all kinds, of events, of the multiplicity of data which surrounds them in the world. The strategies presented here give students a range of choices that put them at the center of their own learning and thinking — making conscious choices, rejecting paths of inquiry that don't produce results, looking critically at the material at hand and at their own ways of dealing with that material. As they practice applying perspectives and thinking critically about those perspectives as interpretive tools, they also learn to step within a framework and see how the world looks from inside and then to step out and turn their critical gaze to the framework itself.

Part Two

Readings for Academic Writing

As the introductory section points out, the six chapters in the second part of the text provide a variety of options for research projects. Depending on your class and your plans, you can take these opportunities in any of several directions. You may choose to work with the whole class on one or more chapters, to allow students to select a chapter to work on individually or in groups, to develop short research units based on several selections within a chapter, or to ask students to move beyond the materials provided to more complex projects.

These chapters provide the opportunity for you to guide students in looking at texts next to one another, in doing research that's quite different from the report writing many are accustomed to. You'll want to remind them of the guiding principle of the earlier chapters: They are trying to develop an interpretive perspective, not simply to restate information or to gather quotes.

Chapter 7

Women and Power (p. 359)

Framing the Issues

You might want to begin this chapter with a prewriting exercise or with some preliminary discussion that orients students to possible lines of development.

One topic for prewriting: When we talk about power, what are we talking about? What forms of power are there? Are some forms of power more fundamental than others? You might ask students to freewrite on this topic, or assign it as a journal entry.

One of the themes emerging from the materials in this chapter is the idea that in cultures where women have (and are perceived as having) economic power, other powers follow. If you would like to orient students to this theme right away, you might open the door with a question like this one: Do you feel the most fundamental human powers are biological, social, or economic? These three are undoubtedly false alternatives, particularly the distinction between *social* and *economic*. But such a question warms up students for what follows.

You might also invite students who have studied cultural anthropology to explain to the class what the field includes and how anthropologists gather data. If your class doesn't include such students, it may fall to you (or, perhaps, a willing colleague) to explain what anthropologists do and how their work differs from other kinds of investigation. This explanation may be brief, but it should orient the students to the material they will read in this chapter.

The overview pieces in Framing the Issues, pages 360–365, can be hard to work with if you spend to much time on them individually; they are apt to flatten out in paraphrase into a few bland generalities. But brought into conversation with one another, disagreements and differences of emphasis start to arise. As quickly as possible, try to get students to compare quote to quote. Which writers seem to say compatible things, and which seem opposed?

One way to get students thinking is to ask them to find a scheme for classifying these quotations. If you try this, it's a good idea to have the class discuss the various schemes they've found; without such discussion, students are sometimes seduced by their own categories as they progress to the other readings. Here are some of the bases students have used for classifying the quotes: feminism/ antifeminism; flexibility/inflexibility of human nature; kind of evidence implied; audience; attitude toward economics; explanations from nature or from culture; writers who stress education and those who do not. We've noticed that asking students to classify all the quotations sometimes distracts them from focusing on two or three quotations about which they have the most to say. This is a situation where classifying may have some heuristic power for generating distinctions but needn't be followed through to completion.

Students may also find it useful to list the words that these pieces emphasize and that they'll want to define in light of their readings in the rest of the chapter: Such words as *status, power, prestige, class,* and *work* come to mind. You and your students will certainly be able to expand this list.

Additionally, suggest that students consider the perspectives not only for the views they present but also for the questions they raise. They can keep a running list of questions in their journals as they do the reading: Who gets and who measures status? Who has power (and what *is* power)? Who or what gives power? What limits or compromises it? How do the size of a country or region, its geography, its relations with surrounding communities, and its degree of industrialization seem to influence the place of women in the society? What mechanisms exist within a society to establish control and to maintain various forms of power? How do traditions and expectations determine power? Do different groups and different individuals interpret power differently? In what ways is it difficult to see another culture accurately? What are the impediments? How is it possible to surmount them? What are the implications of the various views of men and women implied in the quotations that frame the issues? The list is likely to grow as students read and think about the articles in the rest of the chapter. If students have the list to refer to as they think, discuss, and, more important, write, they will be more likely to stay focused on the reading.

One general subject that may need some glossing: Explain that hunting-gathering is presumably the way that humans maintained themselves before the invention of agriculture. Based on contemporary evidence of the few cultures that have been known in modern times to subsist by hunting and gathering, men are more likely than women to be the hunters and women are more likely than men to be the gatherers. Why all the hubbub over hunter-gatherers?

Some further notes on the first group of quotations, pages 360–365: the quotes from Margaret Mead and Simone de Beauvoir prove slippery to compare, partly because de Beauvoir's comments are not informed by, or concerned with, cross-cultural comparison. Unlike most of the others quoted in this section, she is not an anthropologist speaking to other anthropologists. This may account for some stylistic differences too. It can be fun to contrast the forthrightness of what she has to say with the hesitating, larded-over quality of Evans-Pritchard's delivery: "We may come to the conclusion that, taking everything into consideration and on balance, it cannot be said, certainly without many qualifications that . . ." What makes us think this man may be saying something unpleasant?

Evans-Pritchard may be difficult to critique without any anthropological data at our disposal, but the generalizations offered by Washburn and Lancaster are fair game. You might try the following argumentative exercise. First ask students to write out the statement "In a very real sense our intellect, interests, emotions, and basic social life — all are evolutionary products of the success of the hunting adaptation." Then brainstorm as much support as possible for that generalization. Next have people write out a radically altered version of the same statement, changing the thrust entirely (try substituting "gathering" or "motherhood" for "hunting," or in place of "all are evolutionary products of" substitute "all have little to do with"). Then brainstorm support for *that* generalization.

We've found that from a contemporary feminist perspective the passage by Margaret Mead is by far the most difficult to deal with. It's partly because Mead seems to associate all civilized "constructions" with masculinity. True, she sees them as expressions of eternal male insecurities. Women, by contrast, seem to have built-in reasons for complacency, a "sense of irreversible achievement," in childbearing. It takes something "divine," or at least a good dose of education, to shake women into restlessness. You might want to ask your class how they think Ortner might respond to this passage from Mead.

First Passes

These questions ask students to begin to think about specific examples to which the quotes might apply. It's helpful for them to try these exercises before they continue with the rest of the readings so the issues become grounded right away in specific instances. The questions they've already begun to list in their journals should provide a good starting point for the activity suggested in First Pass #3. In addition to expanding the list, they can also think about evidence in light of their own work on the first two assignments.

If you prefer to stop here, you might ask students to write a short essay setting their own experience into one (or more) of the perspectives represented in the quotes. Ask them to try to imagine one (or more) of the writers seeing their experience and deciding how to analyze it. They might start with a dialogue in which two of the writers discuss an experience or an issue raised by the students' observations. If students are working in groups, they might each adopt a perspective and try to speak as that writer in explaining their experiences.

If students are reluctant to look closely at their own experiences, you might consider taping one episode of a popular TV sitcom or drama that deals with the issues raised in the first group of readings. Show the tape in class or ask students to watch it outside of class, and ask them to analyze it from the perspectives represented in the opening quotes. In essays, students could write about how the perspectives help them analyze what they see. They could also determine which perspectives seem to provide the most helpful insights and explain why. As part of the process of analyzing their own experience or some representation of experience in popular culture, students can also begin to think about how we observe, what we see, what we can know, and what we cannot know when we view and try to analyze anything outside ourselves. How are our own views, the lenses through which we perceive and evaluate reality, shaped? If they have worked with the "Analyzing" chapter, students have already begun to think about these questions. If they've kept journals, those reflections may be helpful here.

Complicating the Issues

In general, we find it's both easier and more interesting for students to write about the pieces in this section in combinations, so even if you do a truncated version of the chapter, we'd recommend that you assign at least several articles.

One exception to this advice, and one piece that has been successful in generating rich essays on its own — analytical, autobiographical, journalistic, sociological — is the excerpt about Brady's Bar, *The Cocktail Waitress*, page 418. Many students have ready analogies at hand and can describe workplaces they've known in a layered detail similar to that provided by Spradley and Mann.

From *Iroquois Women: An Ethnohistoric Note* (p. 366)

Judith K. Brown

Judith K. Brown's *Iroquois Women* lends itself well to arguments pursuing the theme of economics. It also provides a glimpse of women as gatherers (although Iroquois society is also agricultural). Although a strong case can be made for a kind of sexual equality among the Iroquois, a strong case can also be made for Mead's point of view — that male's work was defined as different and *therefore* carried prestige. Or did it carry more prestige only among men?

Students might begin by considering what power means in this society. How is power defined in both economic and political spheres? They can look again at Sacks, Leacock, and Mead as they think about these questions.

As students work to make sense of the various sources that Brown uses in making her argument, they may also think about who notices what and how the views differ. Although the variety of source materials may seem confusing to them, students should think about how each observer sees and reports, about the difficulties of knowing and about the way the preconceptions and ideas of the observer shape what is seen and how it is understood. Much of their work in earlier chapters, particularly in "Analyzing" but also in "Classifying" and "Comparing," may have prepared them to work with this difficulty.

!Kung Women: Contrasts in Sexual Egalitarianism in Foraging and Sedentary Contexts (p. 372)

Patricia Draper

Patricia Draper's *!Kung Women* yields interesting comparisons with Brown's piece on the Iroquois. It also contains within itself grounds for comparison between the bush !Kung and the sedentary !Kung. You might focus on page 382 as a particularly revealing episode for what it suggests about gender roles in settled societies. We've also found that Draper's comments on page 380 about sex and architecture are fun to work with.

Many of the readings in Framing the Issues offer interesting connections here; in fact, students working with this piece could probably choose any of the perspectives and consider how it illuminates the article, as well as how, taken alone, it is inadequate as a lens through which to view the !Kung women. If the whole class is working with the material, it might be stimulating to assign perspectives to groups of students, ask them to discuss the connections, and then share the results.

Ask students to think about overtly acknowledged roles and responsibilities and those that are more covert. If they read Constance Cronin's piece on Sicily and Margold and Bellorado's on Palau, they may discover some interesting comparisons and contrasts; they may even be able to extend theses fruitfully to their own experiences and the circumstances they observe around them. The subject might serve as the basis for a provocative essay.

Other questions raised here: Is women's role in the economy the central power issue, or does power in the social organization of a community derive from something else? How does the physical setting influence power and social organization? And what about notions of public and private?

Since the !Kung have been so widely studied, this article provides a possible jumping off point for additional research if you or your students are interested. Although the materials in the chapter function as a self-contained mini-library, you may expand the field with additional materials if time and interest warrant.

Illusion and Reality in Sicily (p. 389)

Constance Cronin

Constance Cronin's *Illusion and Reality in Sicily* cooperates with arguments about male appearances versus female realities or with various arguments about what constitutes social power. Question 10 in Options, about covert sources of women's power, has proven a good vehicle for writing about the lives of Sicilian women as described in this chapter. An interesting research project would be to interview some second- or third-generation Sicilian-Americans: Does Cronin's description of Sicilian culture match their firsthand knowledge? Are male-female relations among Sicilian-Americans subject to unusual cultural pressures?

When people move to another country, are the structures maintained, or are they unique to Sicily? Do their forms change? And what is the role of class in the social structure?

Cronin's phrase "prison of culture," highlighted in the third of the Considerations, might be used as the focal point for an examination of other readings as well. Would students apply the phrase to any of the other readings? And is "prison" a loaded word? Might an outside observer see as "prison" some part of a culture that would not be seen that way by those living inside it?

From Matrilinear Heritage: A Look at the Power of Contemporary Micronesian Women (p. 399)

Jane Margold and Donna Bellorado

This study offers a glimpse of women living in two cultures. As a way of getting started, you might ask students to read this article looking for evidence to support Jane Margold and Donna Bellorado's claim that "the traditional culture in Palau has not been overtaken by the transitional culture . . . . The two cultures coexist side by side."

The cultural — and, more specifically, economic — importance of food is a theme this article shares with Brown's on the Iroquois and Draper's on the !Kung.

This piece is another that lends itself to the question about covert forms of power, but it resists easy equations of the "Palauan women, like Sicilian women . . ." type. The powers of Palauan women are freely acknowledged by the culture as a whole. It could be argued, though, that Palauan women's power does not match their responsibilities. A brief writing assignment "Is Palauan society sexist?" has yielded good responses on both sides of the question. There are also interesting possibilities lurking in the quotation on the bottom of page 401, "I think a woman is more oppressed than a man," implying that *both* women and men are exploited by the "transitional" culture, although to different extents.

One cultural question to be asked of this and the other contemporary cultures described in this chapter: Does there seem to be an active women's movement in this society, and has that movement itself become a significant part of the culture? The answer in the case of Palau: There seem to be signs of feminist awareness but no actual movement — to judge only from this excerpt.

Women Workers in the Mondragon System of Industrial Cooperatives (p. 403)

Sally L. Hacker and Clara Elcorobairutia

The "I" of this piece is Sally L. Hacker, the primary author.

The Mondragon system is an eye-opener for most students, and you may find it necessary to spend some time discussing it. Go over details such as the range of wages and provisions for retirement. "Is it Communist?" students first suspect. Discussion helps to clarify that despite the communal aspects of the system, including the collective ownership of the means of production, the industries themselves turn on profit and market competition. You may also want to discuss the general cultural situation of Basques. They are "semiautonomous," as a highly differentiated cultural group, with their own language and institutions, within (an increasingly liberalized) Spain.

Once the Mondragon system itself is less hazy, you can turn to questions of women's power. It's difficult to get students to read this article with any attention to nuance. One strategy that has worked for us is to break the class into small groups of four to six students. Have half of the members in each group compile support for the belief that women in the Mondragon cooperatives are better off than women in the society at large. Have the other half support the idea that they are not better off. If the interchange gets animated, you might follow up with an assignment that asks students to present Hacker and Elcorobairutia's attitudes in some complexity.

A loaded question that helps students to group much of the material in the article: "If cooperative systems level the differences between rich and poor, why don't they also improve the lives of women?"

Before tackling the information in the midsection of the article, pages 406–411, we've found it helpful to ask students to work from Table 1 on page 407. What tentative conclusions can they draw from those data alone? If they've tried to write about those data (the numbers in parentheses, by the way, indicate total numbers of male and female workers), they will be in much better shape to follow the discussion itself. Interestingly, in the context of that discussion, the data start to look a good deal more ambiguous than they do without such context. Is the fact that 70 percent of the women (or seven women) at the cooperative printing plant are unskilled workers a good or bad thing? How does the last paragraph beginning on page 406 complicate the issue?

Is Hacker's point of view that of a sociologist out to describe social structures and conditions in as neutral a way as possible, or does she write from a political vantage point of her own? We were a bit surprised to discover how many students felt at first that this article, perhaps because of its thick data and distanced language, was value-free. It's worth going through the article once noting explicitly places where Hacker is acknowledging her own feminist assumptions.

From *Women's Work and Chicano Families: Cannery Workers of the Santa Clara Valley* (p. 414)

Patricia Zavella

This excerpt, we realize, starts abruptly. Despite the headnote, students will need some orienting: "What's going on here? To what changes do these women seem to be responding?"

You might ask students to compare the working conditions for women in the American canning industry with those of women in the Basque industries as described by Hacker. For a three-way comparison, you might include the women of Palau.

A question: "Do the Chicanos interviewed by Patricia Zavella encounter more discrimination because they are Mexican-Americans or because they are women?"

Another question: "Can legal changes improve the status of women in sexist cultures, or do cultural changes have to come first?"

To what extent do cultural issues affect the workplace? Is it necessary to take the social structure of a culture into account before establishing programs designed to provide equality in the workplace? To what extent? Or is the aim of such programs to change social structures as well as job opportunities? Where do expectations and traditions fit in?

How does the operation of the canning industry's affirmative action program indicate the gap between a social program in theory and a social program in practice? Do the differences between the ideal and the real make for pessimism about the net influence of such programs?

From *The Cocktail Waitress* (p. 418)

James P. Spradley and Brenda J. Mann

This is the piece that seems to create the most immediate interest and draw out the readiest strands of personal testimony from students. The categorizing and the hierarchical scheme presented in Figure 3 on page 425 provide effective models for students in writing about employment structures they know. In many instances, students describe structures that are far less stratified by sex than the bar scene described by James P. Spradley and Brenda G. Mann. But not always. (As a sidenote about this piece, we can't help but observe the patriarchal structures of the research design: Who did the field work, and who oversaw the project and got top billing?)

You might want to ask a general question about how Spradley and Mann produced their findings. In writing their article, to what extent did they rely on (1) the work of other anthropologists, (2) interviews, (3) firsthand participant-observations, (4) the analysis of data provided from other sources? Number 3 gets the nod, but you'll want to point out that the authors also rely on number 1 in the sense that the strategies of observation and analysis are themselves central to the discipline of anthropology. On page 420, for example, the authors proceed to perform what they call "social network analysis." Ask how we can tell that this strategy is not itself their own invention.

This article provides a fine occasion for asking students to reflect further on the use of classifying in academic writing. The third paragraph offers these illuminating sentences: "These people were more than just customers, as Denise had initially categorized them. Nor could she personalize them and treat each one as a unique individual. They were different *kinds* of people . . . ." Why *can't* she treat them as individuals? we may ask. Perhaps she could, but at what cost to her ability to function? Sorting out the kinds, the authors contend, is the key to learning to understand one's social context. See the final paragraph (p. 435) where this point about cultural categories is highlighted as a major conclusion of the article: "Like a social map, these cultural categories enable the girls to sort people into groups, anticipate their behavior, and plan for dealing with them."

Some lively classroom discussion has turned on the waitresses' categorical treatment of female customers. What are the feminist implications? Are the waitresses' attitudes sexist? What kind of social context set women against women? Look at the authors' hard-boiled analysis on page 435. Have times changed since 1975, when the research was done?

In addition to asking students to write about their own work experiences in Spradley and Mann's terms, you might want to consider asking them to interview their parents or other family members performing "social network analysis" on what they learn. Students have reported some lively family conversations about the working experiences of their families.

Options

As students consider the questions in this section and others raised by their work with the chapter's materials, they may need to be reminded again that their most important task is to develop and work with an interpretive framework. Many students are in the habit of simply quoting a collection of information and opinions from "sources" and of producing a report that has no clear purpose other than to exhibit their diligence in going to a library.

The tasks presented in this chapter ask students to use the strategies they've worked with in the first part of this text: to define terms, to think about how data is gathered, to sort people and behaviors into categories that are useful in expanding their understanding, to compare the perspectives and the studies, as they look for illuminating connections (and disconnections), and to look at one text in the light of another.

You may have them work with the entire chapter or with "mini-units," which you or they design, based on groupings of perspectives and studies centered around issues and questions. If you or they want to move beyond these materials, there are opportunities for fieldwork, for additional library research about the peoples described in the articles or on the theories presented in the first quotes. Students can also move toward the personal, analyzing their own experience in light of the reading they've done here.

At the end students should probably spend a few minutes reflecting on what they've learned — both about women and power and about research. Even if they've written a formal paper of some kind, a less formal journal entry may help them see and understand what they have done.

Chapter 8

Caribbean Fiction (p. 438)

The fiction and commentaries in this chapter are designed to introduce students to the literature of a region that may be unfamiliar to many. Even students who know some of the fiction included here may not be familiar with the whole range of material in this chapter, though they may be able to offer the class additional perspective on a particular area.

You have many options for handling the material in this chapter. Students can work as a class, in groups, individually, or in some combination of these. If you have allowed students to choose a chapter to work on, you may want to suggest that those students who have elected this chapter work together before writing. If the class is working as a whole, consider discussing some of the material together before individual students or small groups select other stories or essays as a basis for their own writing. If the chapter is too lengthy for your class or your course, you might want to work with several of the stories or with a single story and the essay by Catherine Sunshine or with fiction/essay pairs by the same author.

The chapter introduction is intended to familiarize students with the history of the Caribbean region. It is by no means exhaustive. Caribbean students in the class may be able to fill in the outline a bit. And as students read the stories, a bit of historical background research for each country would probably serve them well.

The design of the chapter also allows you to help students see research about fiction in what may be a new way for many of them. Too often, unfortunately, students regard literary research as a process of going to a library, finding an article or a book, and using the idea presented in it as the basis for an essay that simply quotes a critic and a text — the student writer remaining notably absent from the process. The materials in this section are organized to facilitate a process that moves in another direction — from the fiction to the critical material. Students are free to formulate their ideas and observations first, with or without your guidance, and then to read the relevant essays to expand their ideas and illuminate their reading. Because the process described here will be new to many students, they may need your guidance, at least in the beginning.

As students begin to look at the introductory material, you may want to bring (or suggest that they bring) to the classroom some of the typical tourist brochures and publications we've alluded to. Travel books on the region should provide additional helpful material; some of them discuss honestly the history and customs of a region, while others promote features attractive to tourists. A look at this information should orient students to some of the issues that will arise as they read the fiction and the essays: cultural and economic differences, attitudes toward tourists, sense of national identity and pride, family structure, languages, skin color, outside cultural influences, and the colonial past and its continuing influence.

Framing the Issues

To Da-duh, in Memoriam (p. 443)

Paule Marshall

The story may need some contextualizing: Students may not at first be aware of the time frame of the events, of the island's colonial relation to England, and of the labor unrest that was evidently part of the political and economic backdrop. Other historical background becomes evident in the story: the omnipresence of sugar cane, the grandmother Da-duh's independence, the role of Panama Canal work projects in getting the money that enabled her to buy her property, the fact that she seems vaguely aware of white people but rarely has to deal with them, and the British planes at the end.

The tension between the narrator and Da-duh is, perhaps, the most interesting feature of the story for students to analyze. How is it expressed? Their struggle is carried on in words and images, and the climax seems to occur when the girl constructs an overwhelming verbal image of New York. This theme of the power of language runs throughout many of the stories in this chapter.

At the same time, students may want to think about the tense but ultimately affectionate rivalry in which each tries to impress the other with features of her world. The final paragraph of the story is evocative in its image of the girl, now grown, reflecting on her relationship with her grandmother in a setting that combines the machines Da-duh feared most and was most in awe of with the paintings capturing the lush island imagery that was so powerful for both of them. In fact, using this paragraph as the focus of a short essay often helps students think about and interpret many of the story's central themes.

From *Crick Crack Monkey* (p. 450)

Merle Hodge

The background information in the headnote will orient students to the events and issues of the story. They'll be interested, we think, in the way young children are enrolled in school, as well as in the content of the education once they get there. And they'll be amused by Tee's uncomprehending participation in the routines of the school day, seeing (through the eyes of the adult narrator) more than the young child can of the nature of the education she's receiving, of the social setting of the school, of Mr. Hinds's attitude toward his young charges.

Students may be puzzled by the "up there" and "Glory" references at the end of the story. The context of the novel helps: The narrator's mother has died and she is being cared for by her mother's side of the family. But her father is in England ("Glory") and may send for her, much to Tantie's dismay. In the meantime, her father's sister is also making moves to pull Tee (her name is Cynthia) away from her rural relatives. All this accounts for the rage observed in Tantie (p. 456)

A good place to begin might be to ask students to think about the issues motivating the women to rush about trying to get their children into school. Why is the first school most attractive, as far as they can see? In what ways does it seem most in touch with the community, and what does Mr. Thomas's dialect tell us about the school's connection to the people? Why is the Catholic school a second choice? And why is the Hinds's school a distant third? — a question whose answer becomes more and more obvious as the story progresses. In addition to Mr. Hinds's attitude toward his pupils, it's clear that the school's affiliation with the Church of England is part of why it's so undesirable; there seems to be a current of nationalism underlying the parents' point of view.

If you are using both of the first two stories, some comparisons might be in order. Both use an older, more sophisticated narrator recollecting a childhood experience; both portray a woman-centered social world; both register an offstage British colonial power — though in this story the British have a full-fledged emissary in Mr. Hinds.

There is a nice thread of correspondence between the saturation of English literature and lessons in this story and Wordsworth's daffodils as recollected in the excerpt from Jamaica Kincaid's "Mariah" (p. 497). If students have read both stories, see what they make of the connection. Also, what Catherine Sunshine says about parochial schools, particularly on pages 515–516, applies to all the cultural propaganda to which the children in this story are exposed. If your students have worked with the Graff excerpt in "Analyzing," they should see the connection — the moral and cultural content of seemingly objective lessons that becomes propaganda.

If you ask students to pair this piece with Hodge's essay on page 536, they can think about how Hodge's view of what fiction can and should do is reflected here.

My Aunt Gold Teeth (p. 458)

V. S. Naipaul

One of the most fruitful ways into this story may be to ask students how Naipaul and his narrator seem to feel about the characters in the story — and about the conflicts among religious observances that pervade the story. You may find it profitable to combine work with this story with a reading of Naipaul's essay (p. 534) to better understand the almost mocking distance he and his narrator maintain from the characters and events of the story.

If your students are working with several stories, they may find it useful to compare these first three. On the surface these stories seem similar in point of view, being told simultaneously from a child's viewpoint and that of the mature and experienced adult the child has become. And yet students are sure to detect important differences: In Naipaul's story the narrator seems detached even as a child. His clear-sighted, dispassionate recounting of facts and events and his descriptions of characters make him sound alienated. And there is little evidence of the kind of affectionate reevaluation that inspires the paintings of Da-duh's granddaughter or even of the clear affection of the grown-up Tee for the bewildered child she was and for the relatives who tried to do their best for her. This is not to dismiss the obvious criticisms in both stories — the machines in "To Da-duh" and the Hinds's school in *Crick Crack Money*. But the underlying tone is quite different in those stories from the tone that emerges here. If students feel put off by Naipaul's story, invite them to talk about why: What is there in the narrator's voice that has this effect on them and do they think Naipaul has recreated this effect deliberately?

Comedy may be another way into the story: Do students see the story as comic? If so, why? What is the effect, for example, of calling the central character Gold Teeth? Of her religious vacillation? Of the other characters' attitudes toward religion? If students don't sense the story as comic, how do they perceive it? Would "sadly comic" be a good description? Or can they find something even more accurate?

To lead into the issues in the story, consider asking students two questions:

1. What general image of Hinduism does Naipaul's story present? Of Christianity?

2. What does the grandmother say of Gold Teeth's Christian experiments before Rampersad's death? What does she say after? Why do you think Naipaul presents us with these two reactions so close together?

The insularity of the Indian community is striking. Some paragraphs (such as the one that begins "Presbyterianism was not the only danger . . . ") suggest cross-cultural influences in the day-to-day life of these people. Yet we don't really see that influence directly in the story. The characters don't trust doctors either — and Gold Teeth's forays into Christianity only point up how alien that world is to the characters in this one.

In fact, the religious issues may be most interesting to look at with students. The image of Hinduism presented here is rather negative: What, for example, is involved in being a pundit? And what do students make of the Ganesh: "with the license of the mystic, he had exploited the commodiousness of Hinduism." The theme of religious hypocrisy is underscored by the grandmother at the end of the story: "That is why I encouraged Gold Teeth to pray to Christian things . . . I don't like these Christian things."

King Sailor One J'Ouvert Morning (p. 464)

Lawrence Scott

One way to get students writing about this story is to ask them to compose a simple summary of the action of the story: A man comes to Trinidad to participate in Carnival; after some initial nervousness, he does participate and has a good time. This kind of barebones summary, as we discussed in the "Summarizing" chapter, strips the story of vitality and meaning. Ask students to talk about what's missing — and about why the missing elements are important.

Students will probably need a bit of help sorting out the past and present of Philip Managas. What do we know of his background and his family history? What does he remember of his childhood? You may want to suggest that students go through the story once looking for details of Philip's family history. How much can we piece together? Where has he been? Is he staying? Why is he so self-conscious about being mistaken for a tourist? Was he, in a sense, a tourist in his childhood? Where is he now, and how do his past and present connect? Catherine Sunshine will be helpful here (especially p. 520 ff. and p. 523) in contextualizing Carnival and in helping students understand the issues of race and class (pp. 518–521) that cause some of the protagonist's uneasiness.

The native/tourist tension, the conflict between cultures, the search for belonging — all are important themes here. Ask students to look at how Carnival and music figure into Philip's experience. And how are the questions he faces at the beginning of the story — particularly those about his childhood and his social status — answered or left unresolved at the end? The flow of the story, like the flow of Carnival itself, can be seen as purgative. Of what is Philip being purged? Does the purging work?

The paragraph in the middle of page 467 ("There had been envy then too . . . ") may need some explicating. Students need to see that the "then" signals a flashback and that the envy Philip refers to comes out of his not having been allowed to participate in the real Carnival parades but rather having to go with his mother to the sanitized club version, where things British are not mocked but celebrated in the "cute" fashion suggested by Peter Pan and Bristol boards.

If students are thinking about history, you may want to ask them to consider the image of a receding white colonial class that has left Trinidad more democratized but still divided along lines of class and color.

From *Abeng* (p. 469)

Michelle Cliff

The headnote provides salient contextual information for students. As students consider this excerpt from Michelle Cliff's book, they'll want to focus on the attitudes toward tourists, on the history of slavery, on the historical and social context of the events, and on the religions that are central to Clare's experience. How is Clare's experience intimately connected to these issues?

Sunshine's essay (p. 515) should be helpful in its discussion of the distinctions among Christian sects and of the social differences that are an overriding concern of these initial chapters in Cliff's book. In fact, it's fair to say that these background concerns take over the foreground to some extent. We learn who Clare is only against the background of the others to whom she's exposed.

Cliff's narrative is not straightforward; it's more like a mosaic. Perhaps your students can find a better way to characterize the narrative. Do they see a pattern; does each chapter have some kind of climax or a point toward which it has been moving? Do they, for example, see the uncovering of the mass coffin of slaves as the center of Chapter One? And does Chapter Two center on the comparisons among the various versions of Christian worship only to get to the moment when Cliff describes the servant lives of the men and women whose "spaces of need" could not be filled but only "eased" by Sunday services? Or do they see some other pattern or movement? The value of the discussion will lie not so much in the conclusions as in the process of arriving at them.

If your students have read Naipaul's story, they can compare the authors' attitudes toward the characters and toward the religious practices in the two stories.

And while you're on the subject of religion, consider the symbolic overtones of the harpsichord described at the bottom of page 472. What are some of the features it shares with the British presence? Yet how are the Presbyterians different from the Anglicans described in the paragraphs that follow? What does the comparison illuminate — or obscure? And consider the churches on Clare's mother's side of the family (a consideration begun by Clare herself on page 477). Look not only at the Tabernacle but also at the country parish.

Would students agree that Cliff offers a feminist view of Jamaican cultural history? What is that view and which features contribute to it? What, for example, is the contribution to the narrative made by the brief sections about Nanny of the Maroons?

The Two Grandmothers (p. 481)

Olive Senior

If you'd like your students to write about a combination of stories, this one works nicely with Marshall's "To Da-duh" and the chapter from Hodge's *Crick Crack Monkey*. In those stories, the narrator looks back on her own experience from a sophisticated and mature perspective. In the present story, though, the narrator is not yet mature. Her letters offer students an opportunity to look closely at language as it reflects her changing values and to read between the lines to understand the unreliable narrator. Begin by looking at the first letter and at the narrator's reference to Eulalie's "falling." How do they understand that this "fall" has been sexual, though the girl does not? You might want to ask students to assemble a list of moments when the narrator misses something important or fails to see the implications of what she writes. Does the number of items increase or decrease as the story progresses? Do they change in kind? You can also direct students' attention to shifts in language: words that appear early and drop out of her vocabulary and, especially, words that appear toward the end. One example, of course, is that all-American adolescent word *boring,* which pops up and takes over in the fifth section. Also, consider the hair crisis in the sixth section. How is it related to the tensions developing throughout the first five sections?

Students can also write about the changes in values and the social class conflicts that are reflected in the narrator's experience and communicated in her letters. How can they see the changes reflected in specific language the narrator uses? And how are those values reflected in the larger culture? We see here the increase of U.S. influence in the Caribbean: The media is ubiquitous and Miami is only a plane fare away. The suburban grandmother has the force of the mainland behind her side of the struggle. And, as Hodge discusses in her essay, there seems little to counterbalance that influence in the narrator's sense of her own culture. In what ways is the cultural struggle here similar to and different from that in "To Da-duh?"

The theme of the "two grandmothers" or two family lines — particularly when one is "whiter" than the other — occurs in many selections in this chapter: in the Cliff, the Scott, the Hodge, and the Marshall stories, for example. It's a theme rich in social and psychological resonances — perhaps underscored mythologically, too, by the ending of the Cliff excerpt, "In the beginning there had been two sisters . . ." This theme, with reference to any grouping of stories and to one or more of the essays, would make a fine focus for a longer essay. Or you could use it as the focus for an exploratory journal entry that brings together several selections in the chapter.

The Coming of Org — A Prologue (p. 490)

John Robert Lee

The story's three sections provide an interesting, though inconclusive, subject for discussion. How are they related? Storytelling, relations between men and women, the functions of myth are all issues that seem to connect the sections.

Students will want to consider the connections without being lured into easy generalizations that the text doesn't clearly support — such as the idea that Tison has become Papa in Part 3 of the story. If students look closely at the time frame of Part 2, they may see that not enough time has elapsed for Tison to become Papa. You won't want to spend too much time on this sort of detective work, of course, but students should come to realize that the connections aren't simply straight narrative: This happened and then this happened.

As one way to get them to see the connections, students could be invited to define Org, at least insosfar as the text allows such definition. What does meeting Org entail? It's different for everyone, but seems to involve some fundamental shaking of the sense of self. Is meeting Org sexist; does it involve "becoming a man"? What seems to be the social function of the myth of Org? What does it purport to explain? Whom does it keep in line? Does its function in Part 1 seem to be the same as its function in Part 3? As students try to sort out responses to these questions, they'll be grappling with the story's complexity, even if they don't arrive at clear answers.

Students are sometimes interested in the Rasta talk in Part 2. Some will know it already. You might ask in what ways this language expresses a set of political or social values. What are they? Does Tison take them seriously? Does the story? How so?

Cross-cultural influences are demonstrated here, as they are in the other readings in this chapter. How, for example, have French influences survived even after the language has died out of the island? And how does folklore function here? These questions could form the framework for a paper that looks at several of the works in this section as reflections of cross-cultural influences in Caribbean societies.

Mariah (p. 497)

Jamaica Kincaid

The narrator in this story responds to overtures of friendship from her employer in ways some students may find puzzling. As students consider the servant Lucy's background and her present circumstances, they'll want to look at and to characterize her voice. What is that voice? Do students understand Lucy's concerns and the feelings that provoke her rejection of Mariah?

What seems to account for Lucy's anger in the story? What so irritates Lucy about Mariah? And what can't she understand — or does she understand Mariah after all? Is her reaction entirely political, or is there a personal component as well? Many of Kincaid's young female characters react against their mothers. If this theme is of interest to some of your students and if they would like to read a longer work by Kincaid, you might recommend *Annie John*. That novel recapituates several of the themes that are so powerful in this story: the need to move away physically and emotionally from mother (and motherland as well) and the pain of becoming aware of the need for the separation and of the anger.

If your students are looking at the historical theme in this chapter, they can see in this story how history becomes not only cultural but also personal. How does the larger history shape and give tone to the personal history? In fact, this theme is another powerful frame for a longer essay that connects several of the works in the chapter.

If your students have worked with the culture shock pieces in "Analyzing," they might find it interesting to look again at Brink and Saunders and to see how their theory does and does not apply here. What are the pressures of adaptation to another culture? Do students see connections within the story?

Finally, if you'd like your students to approach the story through the lens of a rich passage, consider the following:

> A silence fell between us; it was a deep silence, but not too thick and not too black. Through it we could hear the clink of the cooking utensils as we cooked the fish Mariah's way, under the flames in the oven, a way I did not like. And we could hear the children in the distance screaming — in pain or pleasure, I could not tell.

This paragraph shares much with the story as a whole: the deceptive simplicity of diction, the details, the insistence on distinctions, the willfulness, the competitiveness, the need to represent herself accurately at the risk of pettiness, and the ability to seize an everyday image with great ambivalent psychological resonance.

Visiting (p. 507)

Roger McTair

The stories in this chapter begin and end in Barbados. To whom does the title refer — one character or several? How does the incident at the bar represent the tensions and issues of contemporary Caribbean life? How does it suggest ways in which colonization affects both the self-image of Caribbean people and relations among people from different Caribbean countries?

And, if we look at the story next to "To Da-Duh," how does the image of Barbados shift? How has the economy changed and how are the values different (compare, for example, real cane to calypso double-entendre about cane)? Catherine Sunshine's essay will help students look at calypso's treatment of sex and politics. How do her observations illuminate the reading of this story?

One way into the story is to look at the various strata of island society. Ask students to look again at the characters and to try to characterize them in terms of their niche in society. What do they learn from this angle?

Of course, the title insists that we look at the various senses in which people are visiting. Students are unlikely to miss the obnoxiousness of the tourists and the extent to which the natives defer to it. But are all the visitors like these tourists? What about Solomon? Where does he fit in the scheme of things? How do differences between his "visiting" and the visits of the other tourists underscore the theme of "bridges between islands"?

Jamaica Kincaid's essay in Complicating the Issues will work well in connection with McTair's story. Look at her attitude toward tourists and at her analysis of local governments as well. A short essay or a rough journal entry should help students set these two pieces side by side to see what they can learn from the combination.

First Passes

These questions and suggestions for thinking and writing are intended to focus students' attention on the issues raised in the stories. Though we've already suggested some possible combinations of stories and essays, these questions can be answered based only on a reading of some of the stories (or all, if you prefer to spend some time with this section). As we mentioned earlier, it's a good idea to start students thinking about their own ideas and responses to the fiction before enlarging the context with the essays. That way, students will be free to use the additional readings to expand and illuminate, rather than to limit, their own readings of the texts. One approach is to ask students to list themes that two or more of the stories have in common. One reader's list included such items as cultures in contact and conflict, the role of women, childhood as a lens through which to see society, race/color/class, language, education, leaving/returning/ visiting. Your students can compile their lists individually and then share them to compile a class list with which to approach the readings in the next section.

Complicating the Issues

The readings in this section are intended to serve as perspectives through which to look again at the fiction in the chapter. Each offers a vision of some aspect of Caribbean culture or literature that should make students think again about the stories. You may want your students to read all of these pieces; more likely, you'll want to let them choose or to choose for them those essays that focus on the issues raised by class discussion or by their independent reading of the fiction.

If your students have worked with the fiction in the earlier chapters of this book, you may want to remind them of what they discovered. For example, summary needs a guiding purpose to be effective. That purpose guides the selection of details that the writer includes in a summary. A summary of "To Da-Duh" that is intended to illuminate the sources of tension in the relationship between Da-Duh and the narrator will differ from a summary that focuses on the changes that industrialization is bringing to Barbados.

Students will also benefit from rethinking the other strategies they have used. For example, several of these stories might be grouped around attempts to define religion. And comparison between traditional and modern culture would be a useful way to look at several stories as well. Students might find it useful to list and then to classify themes of the fiction they've read in the chapter or the different ways of dealing with similar issues. And, of course, their work in analyzing will be helpful here in at least two ways: If they use readings from Complicating the Issues, they'll be looking at fiction through a particular lens (or two) and trying to decide how that lens illuminates their reading (and, perhaps, limits it); and if they're working with individual stories or groups of stories, they may find it helpful to recall how they found a useful interpretive framework when they worked with the stories in the "Analyzing" chapter.

Unifying Themes in Caribbean Cultures (p. 515)

Catherine A. Sunshine

Before students read and consider this selection, you may want to discuss with them the headnote statement that Sunshine writes "from the point of view of a historian and political economist critical of Western capitalism." What does this mean and what do they expect her to say? How might someone with a different political bent see and interpret events differently?

Though those considerations are important and should probably be faced squarely, the essay is rich in material that is useful in connection with the fiction. Sunshine's discussion of the connections between Christianity and African religions, for example, should help students focus more clearly on religious issues in many of the stories.

Sunshine's discussion of color and class is also illuminating, as is her look at synthesis and resistance in Caribbean culture. And her look at calypso, reggae, and Rastafarianism should give students the information they need to understand references to and uses of those cultural elements in the stories.

In fact, one useful approach to the Sunshine article is to ask students to look at particular stories through the lens of part of the article and, as the "considerations" suggest, to interpret the story or stories either by applying the perspective or by arguing its inadequacy. Students might read the whole essay once for its overview and then focus on one issue, or, if you prefer, read just a section in connection with the fiction.

If I Could Write This in Fire, I Would Write This in Fire (p. 526)

Michelle Cliff

Cliff's essay is autobiographical, and it raises questions of class and of education similar to those raised by Sunshine. What do students learn about Jamaican history and culture from Cliff and how does that knowledge connect to her fiction and to other stories as well? And how is skin color central to social identification? Students may find worth discussion the social differences caused by gradations of skin color that are discussed here and in other selections in this chapter. Incidentally, the Zoe mentioned here may be the same Zoe who makes her way into Cliff's novel.

A Small Place (p. 529)

Jamaica Kincaid

What is the effect, at the outset, of Kincaid's addressing the reader as "you" and of her growing sarcasm? Ask students how they feel about the way they are categorized here. What picture of Antigua is presented, and how does the writer create the contrasts so central to the essay?

Of course, students can look at this piece next to Kincaid's fiction and also next to McTair's "Visiting." Another angle might involve looking at the theme of anger here and in one or more of the stories in the chapter. How is anger expressed and what seem to be its causes? How does the anger connect to the political and cultural history of the region as well as to the individual experiences of the characters?

Trinidad (p. 534)

V. S. Naipaul

Naipaul's critical attitude is as evident in his nonfiction as in his fiction. What are his perceptions of Trinidad? And how does his story "My Aunt Gold Teeth" reflect his attitudes and his criticisms? If students have read the story first, you might ask them how the essay colors their responses to the story. In fact, if you and your class would like to do a brief experiment, you might ask half the class to read the essay first and the other half to begin with the story. Then students could compare their responses and try to account for them. It should also be interesting to compare Naipaul's and Hodge's perspective on Trinidad. It has been said that Naipaul is as negative about other places as he is about Trinidad. If you would like students to embark upon a short research project at this point, they might look at another of Naipaul's "travel" pieces and see if that assertion is accurate. It might also be fun to think about how he communicates his attitudes and what seems to be their source.

Challenges of the Struggle for Sovereignty: Changing the World versus Writing Stories (p. 536)

Merle Hodge

Merle Hodge's essay offers a useful framework for examining not only the excerpt from her novel *Crick Crack Monkey* but also the rest of the fiction in this chapter — and, indeed, all fiction. Her call for a reclamation of native culture, language, and religion and her statements about the importance of literature in helping all of us shape our view of reality can be applied rather broadly to fiction. How does her view of Caribbean literature counteract the effects of the education that is depicted in the fiction in this chapter? How can "stories" shape people's perception of themselves? Hodge asserts that fiction has been used as a weapon "to subjugate us" because fiction allows us to "read" ourselves, to validate our world, and to see who we are. Elsewhere, Hodge has written of the "phenomenon which is not only Caribbean but Third World — the dual role of the creative writer: artist and political activist/commentator. A large portion of the fiction writers in the Caribbean also commit their talents to the region's ongoing social and political struggles — even those who live outside the Caribbean." How does this statement illuminate both the essay and the fiction in the chapter?

Students may want to look at this powerful lens not only as a way of viewing the fiction in this chapter, but as a way of looking at their experience of all fiction in their own past. Did student read their own culture's fiction, whatever that may be? Do they agree with Hodge's assertions? If so, why? If not, what to do they see as problems in her theory — or points where it does not match their experience?

The Considerations suggest additional ways to use the Hodge essay. You may want to discuss the distinction between "stories" and "the storybook" if you'd like your students to write about that question.

Options

You may want to review these suggestions with your students, pointing out the range of options presented and the different strategies they'd need to employ to complete each project. And you may want to spend a bit of time, before they move out on their own to write, summarizing and reflecting on the central themes of the chapter.

Chapter 9

The Causes and Treatments of Schizophrenia (p. 544)

At the outset, you might want to talk with students about their interest in undertaking the readings in this chapter (or, if you're choosing it for them, the reasons for your choice). The materials lend themselves to a variety of writing projects, for which you can offer varying degrees of guidance. You can undertake the whole chapter, providing students an extensive look at the subject. You can divide the chapter into more manageable units, selecting readings that offer possibilities for shorter essays or exploratory journal entries. You can show students very specifically how to use these materials as if they had done library research, sorting out the issues and framing interesting and powerful connections. Above all, you can show them how to bring order and meaning to a group of sources, guiding them away from the "report" format that many have used in the past — no more than gathering, summarizing, and quoting articles with little thought of an organizing perspective. You might even want to do one or two exercises as a whole class, showing students how to adopt a perspective (familiar to them if you have worked on the "Analyzing" chapter), how to develop a thesis and to incorporate readings in writing about it, how to quote and how to use quotations appropriately in a text.

The chapter topic is likely to generate considerable interest, even in students whose academic interests ordinarily lie far from psychology. Schizophrenia is controversial, and the variety of theoretical approaches provided here gives them an opportunity to grapple with several different points of view about causes, definitions, and treatments. In short, the chapter affords students the opportunity to examine closely the ways people go about trying to understand and deal with the workings of the human mind — particularly when the mind is not functioning as it "should." Therefore, whether students choose the chapter for themselves or you assign it, it should be possible to generate significant interest right from the start.

For a full discussion of ways to group the materials in the chapter, how to break the chapter into manageable chunks, and interesting groupings that vary in length from just a few readings to all the selections, please see "To New Teachers" on pages 8–31 of this manual.

Framing the Issues

We recommend assigning all or some of the case histories before asking students to do much with the two initial overview pieces. In fact, it's probably a good idea to get students writing about some of the case histories before consulting the Sue A. Shapiro piece or the APA description. Ask students to form generalizations based on the case studies alone. Then ask them whether their generalizations hold up, or whether individual differences among the cases overshadow common features.

You may want to take into account that the four case histories are not equally easy to read. *Diane Franklin and John Fraser* are written as conventional case studies. *Ruby Eden,* by contrast, takes dialogue form and reads a bit like a play or a documentary, while *David G.,* in diary form, reads as a rambling, unreliable monologue. You might want to assign the first two, discuss them, and then go on to the other two.

An alternative, or perhaps complementary, approach is to have students freewrite an essay on madness before they read anything in the chapter. With their free associations as backdrop, ask them to do the readings and discuss how these cases conform or fail to conform with their notions.

We've found that once students are caught up in the narratives of the case studies, they are more likely to come back to the initial pieces inquisitively and perceptively. One approach is to ask students to read through the Descriptive Criteria, plugging in appropriate examples wherever they can. Encourage them to use examples to clarify the abstract descriptions. Or better yet, encourage them to use examples to problematize the descriptions. Do any of the criteria apply to all of the cases? Do some apply better than others? When discussions work well, it's possible to call attention to the general issue of how to use — and when to turn away from — categories.

Another approach to the Framing the Issues section is to assign an exploratory essay asking students to illustrate and address the problems of definition. Who can be defined as schizophrenic, and who is? Who gets to do the defining? What range of symptoms are lumped under the single broad label (and here you might want to look ahead to the three thumbnail sketches provided by Nancy C. Andreasen, page 584). What are the consequences of the defining?

While you're on the subject of defining, you might want to look with students at the words listed in the terminology section at the beginning of the chapter. A few minutes devoted to how to think about unfamiliar vocabulary by looking for familiar words or parts of words may help students with terminology in other courses as well. Too often students approach the terminology of a course, whether it be biology or sociology or psychology, by memorizing lists of words without understanding them. Show them, for example, that they know what "dementia" means, that knowing "psycho" will help them with "psychogenic" as well as with "psychology," that "hedonistic" is related to "anhedonia" and that "euphoria" connects to "dysphoria." You might even make a short game of the terms, asking students to find as many connections as they can to words that are already familiar to them, either as part of their general vocabulary or as terms they learned in another course.

When you consider Sue Shapiro's essay, you may want to ask students to classify the various explanations and theories that she presents or to use their serializing skills to examine the changes over time and to look at how a body of knowledge evolves. Again, if they make sense of the changes instead of memorizing them, they may develop skills that will be useful to them in their other studies. Ask them to think about the point of compiling and writing such a historical overview. What can we learn from it? When they look at the diagnostic criteria, they can think about a similar question: What are the purposes of such a list? How do they account for its length? How might it be used — or abused?

The poem by an anonymous schizophrenic patient lends itself to exploratory journal writing and to group sharing of journal entries. What are students' initial responses to the poem? What do they feel and understand about the speaker? If the authorship of the poem was not mentioned at all, how might they have read it differently? Do they see any patterns in the emotions or the images? You might choose to work with the poem first, before turning to the case studies, or last, as a way to wrap up the section before moving on to the readings in Complicating the Issues or before concluding your work with the section.

First Passes

When they approach these assignments, students will benefit from exploratory, messy writing that they share and discuss. If they've worked with the "Defining" chapter, they should be aware of the complexities of writing definitions.

If you prefer to stop here without engaging the readings in Complicating the Issues, you may want to ask students to choose one of the First Passes as the basis for a short essay that is drafted, shared in groups, and then revised to a finished product.

Complicating the Issues

Before students tackle the readings in this section, you might suggest that they pause to list the questions raised by the readings in the first section. Issues of cause and treatment will probably emerge, as will questions about what schizophrenia is. Compile those lists into a master list for the class to keep in mind as they read the various theoretical perspectives in this chapter.

In addition, you may want to discuss with your class the purposes of analysis. If the class has worked with the "Analyzing" chapter, they'll probably remember their reflections on what happens when one looks at data from a particular perspective. How might theoretical discussions help them move from classifying symptoms and noticing their instinctive reactions to considering the larger issues of cause and treatment? How does a particular perspective affect proposals for treatment and analysis of cause? Though they'll be able to respond to that question only sketchily now, they'll want to keep it in mind as they read the rest of the section.

We think it's a good idea to assign one piece of writing, however rough, after the first group of readings (or after an abbreviated version of that group that you select for students). You may want to suggest that students write a set of notes for a review that links the separate essays. You might ask your students to assemble the causes of schizophrenia that they encounter in their reading and then to classify them. They'll probably come easily to a biological/social split; you may want to suggest that *biological* might divide into genetic and environmental, and that multiple causes cannot be overlooked. Which possible causes seem to receive strongest support in the readings? For which possibilities does *cause* seem too strong a word?

Trying to define the word *environment* might be another way into the readings. The word can refer to a physical or biological environment, to family surroundings, to social class. Do students see other possibilities? How does environment seem to be related to schizophrenia?

What Is Schizophrenia? (p. 584)

Nancy C. Andreason

Nancy Andreason presents a biomedical perspective in this essay. Her opening paragraphs remind us that the lens through which one looks determines what one sees, how one reacts, and how one interprets. (Students might be reminded of the Keller and Goodfield pieces in "Analyzing," in which this issue was discussed at length in relation to medical research.) How does Andreason's essay illuminate the differing understandings of schizophrenia and the possibilities for understanding the disease? What questions are raised by the variety of possibilities she touches upon? And how are these possibilities unified — what do they have in common?

The Interaction of Social Class and Other Factors in the Etiology of Schizophrenia (p. 586)

Melvin L. Kohn

Melvin Kohn suggests a different model (you might refer students back to the discussion of *model* in "Defining"). His article provides an especially good opportunity for summary as students examine the options he rejects and those he accepts. This model of summarizing and rejecting the explanations of others as an integral part of arguing one's own position may be helpful to students in their own writing.

How does social class figure into Kohn's analysis of the causes of schizophrenia? What other factors does he see as significant and what interaction among these does he describe? What is meant by *interactive model* and how does the model he develops differ from the others students have read and will read? Do some models seem to students more powerful in explaining schizophrenia — do they detect problems or weaknesses in any? (They may need to keep coming back to this question.) And how do students respond to Kohn's analysis of social class and to his description of lower class life? Are there elements of his description they find inaccurate? This piece is controversial, of course. Encourage students to take Kohn on — to argue with his model and with his portrayal of social class, if they're so inclined. Remind students to ask questions of their reading.

Prospects for the Genetic Analysis of Schizophrenia (p. 592)

Carlos N. Pato, Eric S. Lander, and S. Charles Schultz

Pato et al. offer another perspective — genetic predisposition. Upon what evidence do they base their conclusions? How did they arrive at their conclusions? That question might provide a good opportunity for a brief serializing assignment in which students review the studies that led to their conclusions. How does their theory also support the position that there is no simple answer to the question "What causes schizophrenia?"

Family Issues in Schizophrenia (p. 593)

John F. Thornton

John Thornton further complicates the picture by positing the importance of family in the development of schizophrenia. His article also provides a bridge to the next group of readings by suggesting how the disorder might best be treated. Students might wonder how it is possible, if family structure plays such a central role, that families with more than one child may have only one schizophrenic family member? If they don't wonder, you might direct their attention to the use of the word *more* in describing the correlational studies (p. 595). Is correlation the same as causation? This is an important question for students to address. How is the treatment the researchers suggest related to their view of the causes of the disorder? What is the difference, as they see it, between "education" and "family therapy"?

In turning to issues of treatment presented in the last six pieces, you'll want to encourage students to move back and forth among readings, connecting accounts of treatments to hypotheses about causes. There will be a tendency, of course, to see one treatment versus another, and some lively class discussions can result from students' efforts to argue which therapy is "better," or "more realistic," or "more humane." But keep in mind that these arguments are doomed to frustration if you encourage the impression that, equipped with the materials in this chapter, we are somehow in a position to argue for the demonstrable effectiveness of one therapy over another.

What we can do, however, is use the often emotional quality of the classroom discussions to underline the importance of the theoretical differences. What does psychotherapy address that drug therapy does not? If the causes of schizophrenia were entirely biological, what would that imply about the usefulness of psychotherapy? If schizophrenia is socially rather than physically defined, what does that imply about the possibilities for behavior therapy, which is aimed not at underlying causes but at social maladjustments? If schizophrenia has to do less with individual psychology than with social dysfunction of relationships, then what does that imply about individual psychotherapy versus family therapy?

One of the most mature discoveries lurking in the materials is that *either/or* dichotomies are deceptive. There is usually no need to assume, for instance, that drug treatments make psychotherapy unnecessary, or that family counseling rules out individual counseling, or that strategies of behavior modification are incompatible with other treatments. Rather, what we can encourage students to look for as they evaluate readings is curiosity and flexibility among the experts themselves. At the same time we don't want to discourage gut reactions either: "If someone in my family behaved schizophrenically, I'd consider sending them to talk to someone like _____, but I'd never let them close to _____."

As students consider these pieces about treatment, they'll also want to review the discussions of cause. How does choice of treatment(s) depend upon ideas of causation? Can they pair or group any of the readings in this section of the chapter with those in the first?

"Can We Talk?" The Schizophrenic Patient in Psychotherapy (p. 597)

A Recovering Patient

"Can We Talk?", written by an anonymous recovering patient, should be interesting to students. How was this patient treated? How do students feel about the person who emerges from these pages? You might read this selection in combination with the opening poem — both are voices of the patients themselves rather than of people talking about the patients or using their words selectively to illustrate a point or to flesh out a case study. What difference does that make to students' responses? You might ask them to write a bit in their journals about this question and then to discuss their responses.

Treating the Schizophrenic Individual (p. 602)

Kayla F. Bernheim and Richard R. J. Lewine

Bernheim and Lewine provide an overview of treatments. How do these overlap and build upon one another? And what vision of schizophrenia does each address? What are the advantages and drawbacks of each therapy? For what kinds of patients is each appropriate? How do supportive and expressive psychotherapy differ? Since the distinction between the two is likely to be new to students, they may want to be sure they can articulate it — and also to look at how the two are alike in their methods and assumptions. What are the goals of each kind of treatment?

Process, Psychotherapy, and Schizophrenia (p. 614)

Otto Will

In Will's essay, we see perspective and case study combined. It might be interesting to set this piece next to the patient's account of psychotherapy in "Can We Talk?" Will gives us the therapist's perception of the psychotherapeutic process as well as his analysis of what schizophrenic patients have in common and of how therapy helps them recover. How do psychoanalysts try to help schizophrenics?

Consequences for Therapy (p. 617)

Luc Ciompi

Ciompi's article emphasizes the social dimension of schizophrenia. His statement that schizophrenic persons "do not differ from 'healthy' or 'normal' people in any fundamental respect" is certainly worth discussing. How do students respond to it? Why? What implications does it have for treatment? How does he see "stimulation" as central to schizophrenia and structuring the environment as crucial to treatment? And how does the family figure into the picture? Do students see connections between this article and Thornton's? How does Ciompi's position differ from those who focus primarily on the individual relationship between patient and therapist — the psychotherapeutic model?

A Family Orientation (p. 620)

Jay Haley

Haley continues the focus on family in his "family systems" approach to treatment. The assumption here that communication systems influence and even create thought processes is worth discussing. Haley's analysis of the problem and plan for treatment is very different from those proposed by psychotherapists — or by proponents of using a variety of treatments depending on situation and patient. Students should discuss his hypothesis that leaving home and separating from the family is a crucial time in the lives of young adults, a time when schizophrenia is most likely to appear. His notions of responsibility are also worth discussing: "Where there is madness, there is irresponsible behavior" and "A problem young person is behaving irresponsibly and must be required to take responsibility for his actions." And how do students respond to his use of the term "young eccentrics" as well as to the treatment he proposes?

Haley's piece is also capable of casting earlier pieces, particularly the case studies, in a brighter light. Students may make interesting comparisons between Haley and Will, and they may be able to analyze the cases of John Fraser and Ruby Eden with compassion and insight (see also the discussion of Freud's "Dora," someone who certainly could have profited from a family approach, in "Defining," page 22).

Patients' and Caregivers' Adaptation to Improvement in Schizophrenia (p. 628)

Susan E. Mason, Susan Gingerich, and Samuel G. Siris

As Haley describes the importance of family dynamics to the onset and the treatment of schizophrenia, Mason et al. discuss the ways in which improvement in a patient's condition can negatively affect those around him or her. The notion of equilibrium is common to both articles. What does it mean and how can it be disturbed, according to these authors? And how can a change that we see as positive have a negative effect? Consider the differing definitions of "better" and "worse" — and how the same behavior could be viewed as either, depending on one's perspective. This is a good example of how the perspective can create the interpretation. What do these authors see as the solution to this problem? How is their solution similar to and different from others which have been proposed? How do students respond?

A Framework for the Analysis of Psychotherapeutic Approaches to Schizophrenia (p. 634)

David A. Adler

In the final article in the chapter, Adler provides four perspectives with which to analyze therapy with schizophrenic individuals. Students should identify and explain the four and discuss the differences in definition which they represent, as well as their differing implications for treatment. Are there places where they overlap? And, finally, what difference does the perspective make? (By this time students may anticipate this question and answer it even before it's asked.)

Options

The Options at the end of the chapter offer a variety of possibilities for writing. You'll want to choose, or to allow students to choose, from among these, writing assignments that are appropriate to the time you have available and to the way you've approached the readings.

Before settling into writing, you and your students may want to consider organizing a debate or panel discussion, with individuals or small groups assuming the roles of various theorists represented in the chapter. They might discuss causes, treatments, or both. This kind of summarizing exercise asks students to focus on the differences and similarities among perspectives and to think about how each would respond to the others.

Of course, you can remind students how their work with this chapter calls upon the thinking strategies they explored in the first half of the book: defining terms; classifying behaviors, theories, and treatments; serializing historical changes and treatment plans; summarizing cases and theories; and analyzing in both of the ways presented in that chapter: by finding a perspective from which to think about behavior or by applying a perspective to a particular person's case or to a range of behaviors.

Chapter 10

Apes and Language (p. 643)

This chapter introduces students to the research and the theoretical perspectives surrounding the question "Can apes learn language?" Additionally, it leads them to think about such questions as "What does it mean to learn?" and "What is language?"

You can ask your students to read all the materials or a selection, or you can ask them to work in groups, dividing the material and reporting back to the whole class. The Options at the end of the chapter suggest a wide range of topics for and approaches to writing about these materials, or you can use the First Passes questions as the basis for writing assignments. An abbreviated version of the chapter might include the introduction, the Goodall, Gardner, and Terrace pieces in Framing the Issues and the Linden and O'Sullivan in Complicating the Issues. Or you might ask your students to skim all the pieces in Framing, despite the fact that some of them are rather demanding. They might look, as they read, for answers to these questions: What are the research methods? What are the apes' accomplishments? What are the language issues? What are the scientific challenges? Or you might design a unit in which the students read all of the Framing pieces and then work individually or in groups on the Complicating articles, reporting back to the whole group as a basis for discussion.

No matter which approach you choose, be sure to focus attention on the definitions of *language* that come into play in the design of the research and in the evaluation of its results. If students have worked with the "Defining" chapter, the issues that complicate definition should be familiar to them. In this research, those issues become central.

If your students have read the research reported in "The Sounds of Seal Society" (in "Serializing," p. 131), they may want to consider the differences between interpreting language and teaching it. Do the seals have a language or just a series of sounds? When do sounds become language?

Another possibility: Before they read anything, ask students to freewrite about whether any animals other than humans are capable of language. Do students want to believe that apes are capable of language? Why? Ask them to think about their definition of language and their assumptions about humans and other species. This discussion should be a good lead-in to the materials in the chapter.

If your library has access to a film or video that shows any of these projects in operation, students would benefit from seeing the apes in action. Probably the editing of the film will eliminate the possibility that they can come to an independent judgment of the validity of the research, but they'll certainly benefit from seeing the apes and from watching them use the symbol systems instead of just reading about the research.

As your students read the introduction, you'll want to direct their attention to the issues of language use that are raised here. How do the apes use language, according to the researchers, and why do students think it's important for the researchers to tell us this? Review the list of terms (p. 645) with them briefly, perhaps asking them to give their own examples of each. And ask them to think about the scientific process outlined here. If they have worked with the Thomas (p. 241) and Keller and Goodfield (p. 319) pieces earlier in the course, the notion that scientific research is not a single process that proceeds neatly from beginning to end should sound familiar.

Framing the Issues

In this section, students will meet the famous ape-subjects (and a gorilla) and the researchers whose names are most familiar in the field. This sense of a history, a sequence, and a scientific community should inform their reading of the chapter.

Language Acquisition (p. 646)

Jane Goodall

How does Goodall's own work with chimpanzees differ from the laboratory research reported in the rest of the chapter? If some of your students are interested in that question, they might want to read some of her work. One question to ask of it is how chimpanzees communicate in the wild. Is English (or American Sign Language) a second language for them? Do any communication patterns that Goodall observed parallel what the chimpanzees have been asked to do with language? Any student who is interested — now or later — in looking into that question can report back to the class on what he or she has discovered.

How might Goodall's perspective differ from the perspectives of the others in this chapter? She mentions nothing about the controversy surrounding the language research; what might account for this? How might her interests as a preservationist and environmentalist be served by the language work? Or is the whole subject outside her expertise? Can students see in her work something about how summary functions selectively?

Teaching Sign Language to a Chimpanzee (p. 648)

R. Allen Gardner and Beatrix T. Gardner

This article will introduce students to the methodology of American Sign Language (ASL) training as the Gardners used it with Washoe. Students should pay attention to what the Gardners did and why, to the results of the training, and to their conclusions. Why did they choose ASL? How did they teach Washoe? How did they interpret the learning they saw? What is meant by transfer of training, and what behaviors did they see as representing transfer? You might suggest that students try classifying the items in the table (p. 656–657) and see if they can generalize about the kinds of language tasks in which Washoe was engaged. What do students see as Washoe's most significant accomplishment and why do they call it significant?

What are the requirements of a scientific experiment? How did the Gardners observe those requirements? Did they take measures to protect themselves against criticisms that their work was not objective?

If any students in your class know ASL, ask them about the language. Can they describe the vocabulary, syntax, semantics, and intonation? If no one in the class can help, you might want to invite someone who is familiar with the language to pay a short visit to the class to make the language accessible to students.

Finally, what can students say about Washoe's life during the training? Certainly, she isn't treated as a lab animal. The Gardners point out that the natural sociability of chimpanzees makes them apt subjects for this kind of research; do you see evidence of that in the article?

Language in Chimpanzee? (p. 663)

David Premack

David Premack's work with the chimpanzee Sarah involved an artificial language that Premack created for the research. You might want to ask students not only if his findings corroborate those of the Gardners, but also if his methods make any significant differences. Ask them to try to describe how his language worked: What, exactly, did Sarah have to do? By what criteria did he measure her accomplishment; what, according to Premack, did she learn to do? Students don't have all of Premack's article here. Are some questions left unanswered?

Students who have worked with the "Serializing" chapter may see in Premack's article evidence for the importance of serializing in reporting scientific research. Though the actual process may be messy and recursive, the demands of the scientific community are that the report provide information that would make possible replication of the research; that demand makes serializing crucial to reporting.

Premack points out that "symbolization and transfer both lie at the heart of language learning." What does he mean by this statement and by his further assertion that "neither is instilled by the present training procedures but is a capacity of the organism that is utilized by the training"? How does the idea fit with what students said or wrote earlier about nonhuman species learning language? The idea is one they should hold in mind when they read criticisms of the research.

And while we're on the subject of the critics — you may want to point out the Clever Gretel section (p. 672 ff.) This section, particularly the part about the "dumb" trainer, gives Premack's critics fuel for their arguments. Yet he's aware of what he is suggesting here; he reports his results with integrity, aware that the findings seem somewhat problematic. Can your students suggest reasons why Sarah might not perform as well with trainers who don't know "her language"? Students should keep this section in mind if they read the critics in Complicating the Issues.

How do Premack's experiments seem to differ from the Gardners'? And what do they have in common? What assumptions does each experimenter make about language, how does the method address the assumptions, and how can they tell if they have achieved what they set out to do? How do students respond at this point to the definitions of language and to the assumptions about what constitutes learning?

Lana's Acquisition of Language Skills (p. 674)

Duane Rumbaugh and Timothy V. Gill

Rumbaugh and Gill, in their report on Lana, describe yet another "language" used in chimpanzee research. Theirs is "Yerkish," a system of symbols the apes learn to use at computer consoles. Students might want to look at the variety of so-called languages described so far and to comment on them. Given what this article tells them about Lana's ability to control her environment through the use of these symbols, did she achieve language? Again, keep students thinking about a definition of language that they can revise and rework as they read but that can serve as a theme as they do these readings.

How does correction of error figure into the learning process? And what is the importance of naming things? The researchers suggest that mastery of the abstract concept that things have names is crucial to language; if your students have seen or read *The Miracle Worker*, they may remember that for Helen Keller, the crucial language breakthrough was recognizing that things have names.

And what about conversation? What are its language demands? Do students see in this report evidence that Lana participated in and/or initiated what they (and the researchers) consider conversation? Do they see such evidence in the other research reports? Rumbaugh claims Lana is not only capable of language but of "reading and writing" (p. 676). What does he mean by this? Is language necessary for reading? For writing?

If students have read all three research reports, they can begin to make comparisons. Which of the experiments are most similar? How do design and testing differ? What are the apes asked to do? By what is success measured? Do their explicit or implied definitions of language differ? Do their treatments of the animals differ?

Conversations with a Gorilla (p. 684)

Francine Patterson

Patterson's work with Koko the gorilla has caused controversy because of the way it was reported. If students have worked with the "Analyzing" chapter, they can think again about the ways in which a perspective may illuminate but also limit what can be seen. And, as Goodfield's essay on Anna Brito suggests, people sometimes hear only in ways they're already accustomed to hearing; when information comes in an unaccustomed form, people may not recognize it. Do students think this may be the case here, or do they see actual problems with the research or the reporting? How does Koko use language? What are the similarities and differences among Koko, Lana, Sarah, and Washoe?

What makes this piece different from the others? Is it more or less persuasive? Are any of its claims or evidence stronger than those of the other pieces? And how do Koko's accomplishments, leaving aside the issue of verifiability, further tax efforts to define language as exclusively human?

What connections does Patterson make between Koko's language learning and that of children? This is a theme that recurs in talking about the ape research. What are the parallels and how are they used to interpret the ape data? Do you and your students see these parallels as valid and helpful? Suggest that students hold this point in mind as they read the rest of the chapter and as they review the other research.

First Passes

These questions appear to have the potential to produce a lengthy essay — or even more than one. They needn't, though. You could simply ask students to come up with a summary and talk about how theirs differs from Goodall's. If they have been talking about the research, the comparison shouldn't necessarily be new ground and could be developed through discussion or collaborative writing rather than in formal essay. Students might keep a running log of definition in their journals; this would be a good time to share and discuss what they've come up with and which questions remain unanswered. In other words, you can make this as large or as small a project as you choose. We think, though, that students should take a bit of time now to talk about the issues raised in the research before they go on to consider some or all of the essays in Complicating the Issues.

Complicating the Issues

What questions are raised by the ape language research? Students might begin here by formulating their own list and then seeing how the readings address the questions they have raised. The introduction to the section suggests the range of objections to the research and conclusions contained here. Students should get a sense of the lively debate, acrimonious at times, that surrounds this subject — a scientific community at work (though unity may be noticeably absent). What assumptions about research and evaluation do all these writers share? What questions do they raise about research, about language, about our fundamental assumptions about what makes us human? It will probably be easier for students to grasp the issues if you work with these essays — however many you choose to ask students to read — individually or in pairs to avoid blurring the positions. You might even consider organizing minidebates in class (Gardnerites vs. Terraceites, for example).

How Nim Chimpsky Changed My Mind (p. 691)

Herbert Terrace

This is the central critical piece in the chapter; through it, students should come to understand what the controversy is all about. The other readings will expand the discussion, offering additional arguments. Terrace is at the center of the controversy, though; if your students read even one piece in this section, this one should be it.

What had Terrace hoped to find in his research with Nim? How did he design the research? And what did he actually find — or, more accurately, what does he think he found? (Others will disagree that he actually found what he describes here.) That, of course, is an important question in all this research: How do researchers know what they've found (before they can even consider what it means)? What made Terrace turn against his own expectations and conclusions? Why does he see the removal of Nim as crucial to his discoveries? How did the videotapes figure into his analysis? How do they make for richer data than transcripts, and how might they, too, be limited?

What abilities did Nim apparently develop? How did Terrace come to doubt and finally contradict his own findings — and those of all the other researchers as well? Is he guilty of overgeneralizing from one instance, or does his criticism seem valid? How does Terrace use children's language learning in his discussion? What do comparisons with studies of language acquisition in children enable him to say about apes? Would other researchers see these comparisons differently? How do your students see them?

You might want to take a few minutes to get students thinking about Terrace's generalization (p. 693) "human language is most distinctive because of its use of sentences." Why aren't individual words and phrases as remarkable as sentences? Your students may need you to point out that each word is a discrete piece of learning, whereas sentences are structures capable of infinite combinations.

How does Terrace's description of context minimize the significance of Washoe's famous utterance "baby in my drink"? (See Linden, p. 709.) This section of the essay might be used as a starting point for finding other examples of how evidence begins to look different when looked at through a wider lens. Might the same effect happen to Terrace's own research? Does it in fact happen in later essays in this section?

Performing Animals: Secrets of the Trade (p. 701)

Thomas Sebeok and Jean Umiker-Sebeok

On what basis do the authors call into question the language research? How do different people interpret the same data differently — and what is the importance of this process? Instead of looking at the ape research as something new, Sebeok and Umiker-Sebeok see it as part of a long tradition of animal chicanery. The "Clever Hans" phenomenon (explained in the Gardners' article on p. 729) is something the researchers knew about and tried to guard against. Students may be familiar with the story but not with the ways it's used in research.

Sebeok and Umiker-Sebeok's criticism of the Gardners' "doubleblind" experimental design is couched in interesting language: Notice its dependence on hedge phrases such as "it is conceivable," "could," "another possibility," and "may have had." The criticism begins to sound like an almost grudging respect for the Gardners' experiment.

How do students respond to Sebeok and Umiker-Sebeok's criticisms?

From *Language and the Problems of Knowledge* (p. 707)

Noam Chomsky

If nothing else, students should be interested in this essay to hear the theories of Nim's namesake! Chomsky asserts that "other organisms have their own systems of communication, but these have properties radically different from human language . . ." Do students agree that the items in Chomsky's list of functions are not present in animal communication? Would any evidence in the research reports challenge his theories? To consider language uniquely human is to dismiss the ape research. How do students respond to this position — does it match or differ from their own positions in response to the questions about animal language at the very beginning of the chapter?

How does Chomsky use studies of language in children to support his theory about language in other species? If the language instinct is fundamental to human beings, as Chomsky suggests, does this eliminate the possibility of apes acquiring language? Chomsky argues that language is the great divide among species; it is not possible in other species. How does his position compare with Terrace's? Certainly Terrace started from a different place — without an assumption that language was impossible for apes.

The Quagmire (p. 709)

Eugene Linden

The questions in Considerations point students to ways of thinking about the complexity of Linden's position. You might ask students to attempt a balanced summary that characterizes his attitude. If the first three pieces in the section have left students feeling that the language question has been settled, Linden should ask them to rethink — and, perhaps uncomfortably, to acknowledge that something called "truth" may not be so easy to arrive at.

Acknowledging the difficulty of defining language, Linden also discusses the difficulty of knowing what is a fact. This discussion may be worth a bit of students' time, since many will have difficulty imagining how a fact can be anything but a fact. Why does Linden title his article "The Quagmire"?

How does Linden call Terrace's conclusions into question? In fact, how does Terrace's own research become a vehicle for criticisms of his conclusions? How does Linden's account of Terrace's research set-up differ from Terrace's own (pp. 695–698)? And what about the section on the "interruptions" issue (p. 713)? Take another look at Terrace's account on p. 692 and compare it with the way the Gardners' graduate student analyzed Terrace's analysis. What do students conclude from all this?

Is Linden concerned with what has happened to the apes that were research subjects? Should we be? Ask students to think about the title of his book, *Silent Partners*, and the remarks with which he closes this excerpt. If students are intrigued by this issue, they might even consider reading Linden's book and using it as the basis for a report to the class or an essay.

Communicative Context and Linguistic Competence: The Effects of Social Setting on a Chimpanzee's Conversational Skill (p. 716)

Chris O'Sullivan and Carey Page Yeager

Nim appears again, this time in a different setting, after Terrace returned him to his original home in Oklahoma. These researchers report finding that testing conditions affect performance and that, in studies of children, asking children to name things instead of to engage in real conversation results in lower levels of language performance. How do these researchers use research into children's acquisition of language? They raise questions about whether "conclusions about conversational skills can be drawn from an analysis of interactions that are more didactic than sociable." How did they study apes in light of these ideas? How do you respond to their conclusions? Is conversation central to language?

If you'd like to have some fun, have some of your students tell the story from the ape's point of view (Option *6) — using Terrace's and Linden's pieces as well as this one. After all the reading of serious research — and this piece certainly belongs in that category, despite its comic moments — an acknowledgment of the comedy seems appropriate.

The Role of Cross-Fostering in Sign Language Studies of Chimpanzees (p. 725)

R. Allen Gardner and Beatrix T. Gardner

As the headnote for the article points out, the Gardners have continued their work, undeterred by criticism. What evidence is there in the article that they are aware of the criticism? This article reports their new research and brings us back to Washoe. Are there significant differences between this research report and the one that appears earlier in the chapter?

On page 734 the Gardners report their studies of how chimpanzees "inflect" individual words; students may need some help with the statements about "the modulation of meaning." But what, exactly is a modulation? Could we call every imprecise sign a modulation?

The Gardners articulate here their assumption that "there is no discontinuity between verbal behavior and the rest of human behavior, or between human behavior and the rest of animal behavior." This is the heart of the controversy: Others insist that there is a fundamental discontinuity between animal and human behavior and that, therefore, animals cannot acquire language as we know it. Lewin continues this discussion of those who believe in "a cognitive continuum" and those of the "discontinuity school."

They describe Washoe's language competence in terms that go well beyond repetition or imitation of sounds or words, and they point to instances of communication among animals in the wild. And they recount an experiment in which Washoe and other apes actually taught signing to Loulis, a ten-month-old chimpanzee whom Washoe adopted, without any human intervention. Students may object to the experimental design, considering it cruel. How do they respond to its design and conclusions? Does it seem cruel only if we assume the apes have language? Do students wonder why the videotape has not been made widely available when it should provide evidence different in kind from other evidences of language behavior?

The sign language acquired by chimpanzees becomes, the Gardners assert, "a permanent and robust aspect of their behavior," not a trick or a temporary skill. The communication skills that the apes learn fit with their natural abilities and communication patterns. How do the definitions of language with which the Gardners are working here shape the study? And, in a larger sense, how does a definition of language expand or limit the possibilities for studying ape language?

The Considerations ask students to look carefully at the beginning and the end of the article and to think about what the Gardners are saying there. How do those sections frame the specifics of the rest of the article?

How do the Gardners relate studies of children's language to their continuing work with apes? Students might want to collect in their journals all these discussions of child language studies and to see how and why they're used.

The article concludes with remarks about issues of definition. In fact, definition is critical to all the work of this chapter. If you have worked on that chapter, now might be a good time for review.

Look Who's Talking Now (p. 739)

Roger Lewin

Lewin's article updates the research at the Yerkes Primate Research Center in Atlanta. His summary reviews the history of the studies and sets the materials in context, reflecting the subject's history, the differences of opinion and interpretation, and the nature of a scientific community.

If you have thought about classifying with your class, you might want to consider Lewin's powerful classifying move as he sorts all participants into the "continuity" and "discontinuity" schools. This strategy is reminiscent of Leonard Silk's classifying economists by means of a dichotomizing strategy.

What does Lewin mean by "a cognitive substrate," and how does that concept figure into the work at hand? Why does Kanzi seem to have more language potential than the other apes studied so far — and, again, what do we mean by "language"?

Options

As we said earlier in the chapter, the Options offer a wide range of possibilities for all kinds of writing. Review the list with your students, if you'd like, and then allow them to choose subjects for individual, small group, or whole class work. Or assign the subjects you'd most like them to write about. The length of the essay, as well as whether or not it requires any outside research, is completely up to you, depending on how much time you have available for this unit. And you'll probably want your students to share what they have thought about and written. A research forum day might provide a great opportunity to review the central questions of the unit: What is language? Can nonhuman species acquire language? And, what does it mean to learn?

Chapter 11

Field Research: What's Funny? (p. 749)

This is the first of two chapters on field research. The work of the chapter revolves around data students collect, consider, and, perhaps, analyze in light of the readings collected in Complicating the Issues. You'll want to discuss with students how they'll collect their data and how they'll work with it. You may even need to explain what field research is. If they've worked with "Women and Power," Chapter 7, the comparison with the anthropological studies presented there will be obvious.

Caution students to work on collecting data over a period of time; if they try to do it all at once, they're likely to run into problems. You can set aside class time to talk about what they're finding. You might even suggest or assign research partners within the class so students can help one another with the collecting and with thinking about what they have found. However you decide to approach the work, we urge you to have fun with it!

You and your students can approach this chapter in a number of ways. Students can work only with Framing the Issues, collecting a variety of examples of the comic and discussing them in class. This approach might include several short pieces of writing and, perhaps, a longer paper (which might emerge from work with the questions in First Passes or from questions the students generate in discussion). Or they can examine their collected data in light of one, several, or all the readings in Complicating the Issues. They might choose one or two of those readings as a frame for analyzing several examples of comedy they have collected, or they might write about one of the Options at the end of the chapter. The project may involve several weeks of class time or just a day or two when students share their findings.

The project might even stretch over the semester, if you choose to assign the unit close to the start of the course and then allow students to return to it as they work with the various thinking strategies. They might, for example, apply their work in "Defining" to developing a tentative definition of the comic. They could use summarizing to help them work with the readings in Complicating the Issues. They could serialize the stages of jokes or comic movies or the ways in which stand-up comics present their routines — or they could look at how most effectively to serialize fieldwork (examining the process rather than just the content). Classifying could help them sort their observations into tentative categories, which they might then compare with the categories developed by the authors in Complicating the Issues. And they could use analyzing in two ways: to develop their own perspective for writing interpretively about what they have observed or to use the readings as a set of perspectives through which to look at what they have observed. In short, you could use this chapter as a small piece of your course, or as a central focus, or as anything in between.

Framing the Issues

As students consider the introductory section of the chapter, encourage them to pose questions that will guide their investigation. They won't want to limit the possibilities, of course, nor will they want to assume they know all the answers before they begin, but they're likely to get more interested if they talk for a bit about why they're looking at comedy and what they think they might find. You should probably also keep in mind (and warn students when the time seems right — which may not be at the beginning!) that talking and thinking about comedy may work against spontaneous comic moments in the classroom. Though your work with the chapter is likely to include genuinely funny moments, some of the most valuable work is likely to feel pretty serious.

As for apportioning the material, you and your students can decide what will work best. If students are working individually, they might want to select several units (including, as the text suggests, "The Comedy of the Everyday"). But if the entire class is working on the unit, you might want to ask small groups of students to work with two units each (again including "Everyday"). If you're planning to take class time to deal with the material, each group might be responsible for sharing their findings with the whole class, and the whole group could then work together to find commonalties and differences. More likely, you'll want individuals or small groups of students to work with several units. Whatever approach you choose, asking students to share their observations, to bring jokes, tapes of sitcoms or of comedians' televised stand-up routines or of scenes from movies will certainly make the classroom more fun. If some of your students are aspiring comedians, they might even perform their own stand-up routines for the class and then join in a discussion of what happened. This possibility may apply to only a very few students, though.

As they share findings, students might begin to talk about their own responses to the humor they have found. Does everyone think the same things are funny? Are there identifiable differences? Are there moments when some students are visibly troubled by what others present? And are there times when the whole class agrees that something is uproariously funny? If they can begin to talk about those instances, they'll be better prepared both to write an essay, if you're doing that first, and to read the essays in Complicating the Issues.

First Passes

The questions in First Passes may be used either as preliminary focal points for the material students have gathered or as the basis for extended writing if you prefer not to go on to the next section. If you'd like to extend the assignment, include interviews or surveys as part of the analysis. Students might share what they've found with others and ask for responses, or they might use others as sources of additional material or of critical perspectives. How do class, gender, and ethnicity figure into humor? Why is comedy so often unexamined, and what complicates investigation? What might they learn about changes in taste over time; would older examples in each category be helpful to collect? And what about the social context of humor? Do they see evidence that different people or groups laugh at different things? Or that people are willing to laugh in some situations but not in others?

Complicating the Issues

The readings in this section are intended to expand students' understanding of what they have been doing. The questions posed here should help them look again at the material they've gathered and analyze it from a variety of perspectives. And the material they've gathered should help them read these essays more critically and perceptively, asking "Does this explain or limit?" and "Does this ring true?"

From *Laughter* (p. 754)

Henri Bergson

This piece is tough going and should be dealt with patiently. Get ready to spend some time looking for examples and working sympathetically with Bergson's generalizations. It's wonderful to reach the point where students start quarreling with Bergson's generalizations, finding them inadequate to account for many comic moments. But students may rush to disagree with this sentence or that sentence before coming to some reasonable appreciation of how much laughter Bergson *does* explain.

And how do students respond to Bergson's theory that the comic "appeals to intelligence" and that laughter is accompanied by "the absence of feeling"? They may want to try to examine their own responses to something comic to test Bergson's theory.

The Logic of Laughter (p. 758)

Arthur Koestler

Arthur Koestler's central idea will need some explaining. The "M_1" and "M_2" explanation on page 759 and the diagram on page 760 are a bit intimidating — perhaps unnecessarily so. Koestler's concept of "bisociation" can be approached through the model of analysis presented earlier in this book: Comic moments occur when a fresh analytical frame is suddenly brought to bear on a situation we had initially framed in some other way. Usually that new perspective has been latent to the situation, but only at the comic moment does it flash overtly into view.

Because Koestler is interested in creativity, his interest runs toward some forms of comedy more than others. He's particularly attracted to puns and other forms of double meanings, especially metaphor. Although his bisociation idea is of more general applicability, his examples tend toward jokes that turn on some double perception of particular language, such as a literal and a figurative interpretation of a word (as in his "turncoat" example).

Koestler divides his comments into issues of logic and style. Jokes and other forms of comedy could conform to his principle of bisociation and still not be funny. His three criteria for successful jokes — originality, emphasis, and economy — seem to shade into one another. In fact, Koestler seems reluctant to stick with these terms. You might ask students to find the synonyms Koestler offers for these three terms (originality = surprise; emphasis = suggestiveness;

economy = implication). "Suggestiveness" and "implication" sound very similar, but Koestler treats them as opposites. Ask students to explain this peculiar terminology. By "suggestiveness" Koestler means all that a comic does to familiarize us with what is coming — we don't know exactly what is gong to happen, but we know something of the climate into which we have entered; we're alert and anticipating, so that when the joke "bisociates" we are prepared to receive the new meaning. By "implication," Koestler means all the work a jokester leaves to her audience, so that we are left with the sense that we are participating in forming the joke's meaning. Suggestiveness insists; implication entices.

Ask students how Koestler differentiates comedy from tragedy — and what he sees as the close connection between them. In the last paragraph of the excerpt, Koestler makes statements about how language works in comedy. How does this description of "economy" fit the examples Koestler has given us, and how does it fit the material students have collected?

From *Rationale of the Dirty Joke* (p. 763)

Gerson Legman

A spirited reading of Legman's opening paragraph is a good way to make a class alert. Ask them what he means by a dirty joke's "ambiguity of purpose."

The phrase "dirty jokes" is sometimes treated as a euphemism for "sexual jokes." Why does Legman insist that dirty jokes really are dirty? They express our terrified awareness of our bodies as things.

Along about the third paragraph, your students may start to wonder "Why does this man collect dirty jokes? He seems to hate them." We don't have the answer to that one either.

Like Bergson, Legman discusses the social function of jokes and laughter. But how does the society that Legman invokes differ from that implied by Bergson? Bergson's idea that laughter helps us to live well contrasts forcibly in emphasis with Legman's view that laughter enables us at best to slough off terror.

Legman's idea that jokes express neuroses is conventionally Freudian. you might even want to connect Legman's view of jokes with our brief quotation of Freud on aggression in "Analyzing," Option Assignment, page 316.

One question to keep bringing to mind: Which of Legman's generalizations work for most humor and which only for "dirty" jokes?

Legman looks at both the teller of and the listener to the joke. What does he say about each and how do students respond to his ideas? Does the material they've collected support his assertion that jokes are "a disguised aggression or verbal assault" that "originate as hostile impulses of free-floating aggression in the tellers . . . as a response to or an expression of social and sexual anxieties they are otherwise unable to absorb or express"? Even if they dismiss his theories as limited, do they see some instances in which his discussion provides powerful analysis of something they've observed?

"Sick" Jokes: Coping with the Horror (p. 765)

Steve Emmons

Do your students have access to joke networks like those he describes? Or is his article misleading in the image it creates? An alternative exercise is simply to have students collect a genre of jokes that do seem in some kind of vogue. What central feature do they share? What other generalizations can be made about them?

This piece is one of several that allow you to introduce the question of humor's relation to anxiety (see p. 767). How much of the comedy in the other examples you've looked at as a class thus far introduces some form of human anxiety that we'd like to keep at arm's length? The point emerges that comedy needs to maintain at least some distance toward these anxieties — or nothing is funny.

The Emmons piece introduces the work of Alan Dundes, a folklorist whose work on comic folklore is very much worth exploring. As a research assignment, you might ask students to locate and report on one or more of his collections and commentaries. What does a folklorist's approach to comedy seem to involve?

How well do these two quotations from Dundes hold up?

All humor is based on tragedy.

In most humor, somebody's in trouble.

You might want to talk about the vast difference between these two kinds of claims. Why would the second quote be hard to disagree with, while the first quote might serve to fuel an interesting counterargument?

Students may want to think about why some people are offended by notions that sick humor helps people cope with anxieties, that certain jokes may be told but not written, and that all humor is based on tragedy. What connections can students make between Emmons and Legman? Are there ways in which the two are significantly different?

History, Chicano Joking, and the Varieties of Higher Education (p. 769)

José E. Limón

Limón parallels other theorists in this section by suggesting that jokes fulfill some very specific functions — but he points to social rather than purely psychological functions. In the material students have collected — not just jokes but other materials as well — do they see examples that reflect the issues Limón raises here? How do jokes (or, more broadly, comedy) "challenge and subvert the accepted social order"? In the materials students have found, do they find any examples of comedy that parallel those Limón writes about but that deal with different ethnic groups — or, perhaps, with class or gender issues instead?

Getting It

Regina Barreca

Barreca's piece can certainly be connected to Limón's. How does humor reflect gender differences and comment on the social order? And do students see connections to their own experiences in Barreca's assertions that men and women laugh at different things? If they have presented in class some of the material they've gathered, did they notice reactions parallel to those Barreca describes? If not, can they account for the differences in any way other than simply dismissing her theory? And how do they respond to the idea that humor can be "dangerous"? Have they encountered political issues in the humor they found? Would they call any of it dangerous? Do they see humor as serving psychological or social functions, or both? Or do different settings and different situations ask comedy to serve different functions?

Options

If your class has gathered and shared examples of humor in the several categories suggested at the beginning of this chapter and has read some or all of the essays, these Options suggest a range of perspectives for writing about the issues.

Whatever you and your students choose, their essays could benefit from preliminary exploratory discussion: You might devote a class session to having students present their ideas to the whole class or to smaller groups (depending on class size and the amount of time you have available). If they can get feedback — questions, discussion, additional information — before they write, the essays are likely to be stronger. Or you might prefer a seminar-like sharing at the end. If you have used the chapter as an exercise in class collaboration, it's probably a good idea to use the final essays in the same way; students will be eager to hear what others have concluded.

Chapter 12

Field Research: Exploring the Discourse of Your Major (p. 775)

The second of the fieldwork chapters provides students an opportunity to gather information and to think about their choice of a major. As in Chapter 11, you and your students have a range of possibilities in how to deal with the research material. You could work with the chapter as a unit toward the end of the semester, or you could make it a semester-long project. In either case, students should probably begin to collect data early in the semester so they have enough time to find what they need.

They could gather the data as outlined in Framing the Issues and base essays on what they find, writing either about questions of their own choosing or about one or more of the First Passes. This data could be shared and discussed in small groups or in a whole-class setting. Students working within the same major might even work together during the collecting stage so they can find and look at a wider range of information than one student could assemble working alone. And the class could certainly benefit from hearing about the differences among majors, the range of discourse styles which students discover, and alternative ways of looking at and analyzing the data they have collected.

As an alternative to researching a major, you might use the materials in this chapter to allow students to explore any department or program of their choice, or even to look at how your school as a whole is structured and how its parts work together. If you choose this latter option, your students can expect to emerge with a firmer knowledge of how the school works, who does what, how to find what they need, how the parts interrelate — in short, how to make their way around the institution. We mention this option in some detail at the start of the chapter because it's an alternative to the more focused field research suggested within the chapter itself and because if you choose it, you'll probably need to work with students to reshape some of the data gathering tasks (though, on the whole, they'll adapt nicely to any approach you choose).

As students are collecting their data, you'll want to find a way to check on their progress. This might be very informal — a look at journal entries, a brief conference or class discussion to see what's happening and what problems students are encountering. They may need some help, for example, figuring out how to characterize the language they're hearing in various settings (lecture, tutoring session, informal discussion in the cafeteria) or deciding how to record all the data they're collecting. For further suggestions, see "To New Teachers" (pp. 8–31).

If your students have worked or will work with Chapter 7, "Women and Power," you might draw the parallels between the research they're doing here and the research the writers did before writing the articles reprinted in that chapter. The comparison is helpful in two ways: Looking at the "professional" analysis of data may help students see ways to think about their own research, and looking at the methodological and interpretive issues they're confronting should help students read the anthropologists' work more perceptively.

If your students are beginning their data collection early in the semester, they can gradually make connections and apply the strategies they are learning in the first half of the book. They might, for example, look at defining terms such as *major* as those words apply to your school and other institutions; summarizing the readings they do, as well as their own observing sessions (it may be new for students to think of a class or a tutoring session as a kind of text that can be summarized and to which they can apply the principles of focus and selectivity which they consider in the "Summarizing" chapter); serializing the coursework and levels of discourse associated with lower and upper level courses in the major; classifying the approaches and tasks which constitute the major; comparing their chosen field with those of other students and comparing approaches within the settings they investigate; analyzing their data in light of the texts they read in this chapter and in light of the perspectives they discover through reading and interviewing in their field.

Your first class discussions of the chapter might, in fact, focus on the opening section as you and your students brainstorm the possible kinds of exploration available to them. Consider with them the idea that language can be a barrier, and ask for examples from their own experience. Allow them to brainstorm, in small groups or as a whole class, about the pros and cons of each area they're thinking about researching.

Framing the Issues

As students begin to do their research, talk with them about the three perspectives outlined at the start of the chapter. Depending on your class, you might allow them to practice interviewing one another, to help each other design interview questions, or to share names of people to interview. And you might helpfully spend a little class time reviewing the lists of activities with your students, answering any questions that pop into their minds. If you're checking their progress along the way, ask them to share what they are doing and what they are finding, as well as any problems they have encountered. Often, just talking about the issues can help students find ways around difficulties, and it's good for them to discover that the class itself forms an important resource upon which they can draw for their work.

Views from Outside the Discipline

If students tackle more than one item from this list, suggest that they compare different kinds of information. The college catalogue or an advising session may yield something quite different from folk wisdom or a survey, for example. It's not a bad idea to encourage students to actually visit the departments to talk about the majors, in addition to talking with a general advisor, if those are used at your school. And an article by or an interview of someone who is not now at the school will provide yet another perspective. If you're assigning the work with deadlines, you might want to use part of a class session after students have completed this phase of their work to summarize what they've done, to share ideas, and to focus the next stage.

Views from Inside the Discipline

If students attend a lecture or two and are ready to talk about the assumptions and the language of the lecture, you might help them find a way into this kind of analysis by looking at the language, assumptions, participation, and presentation style of your class. In the same way, you might look with them at this textbook or other composition textbooks as a way to introduce the idea of how the questions might be used.

Students might also be encouraged to talk about how their presence might affect (or not affect) what happens at a tutoring session or conference and how to be unobtrusive. They might also want to talk with the participants after the session; often the answer to a question such as "What did you see happening here?" might yield interpretations different from the observer's.

Views from Further Inside the Discipline

These suggestions lead students to sources that may be new to many. They may need some encouragement to talk to librarians and to attend public lectures. If your students are familiar with one another's subjects, they'll be able to share notices of lectures and conferences and, perhaps, to attend in pairs or small groups. If your school does not have a graduate school (or a graduate department appropriate to a particular student's research), suggest that students visit nearby schools or write for information. And if they look at dissertation abstracts, encourage them to see not only what areas are of current interest but also what kinds of research are done in the field and how research is reported.

First Passes

These questions are designed to help students focus their research, look again at the data they have collected, and make some generalizations and connections. You may want to have them write journal entries or rough essays at this point or to assemble their work in a more formal way. Students might choose one, two, or all three of the suggested tasks, depending on your preference.

This is a fine time to share their research in a class forum; you might organize around groups who have worked on the same or similar majors (science day, business day, humanities day, for instance), or you might prefer individual presentations. If students are going to continue their work by reading the essays in Complicating the Issues, you might want to delay on the forum until the end of the project and do a more informal sharing now.

If students are preparing to read some or all of the essays in Complicating the Issues at this point, ask them to compile a list of questions that have been raised by their research — questions not just about their respective majors but about education in general, about undergraduate and graduate education in particular, and about American colleges and universities — and then to look at the essays for responses to those questions. If they have already read one or more of the essays, this might be a good time for some preliminary discussion of how the readings connect (or don't) to the research they've done.

Complicating the Issues

The range of materials in this section is intended, as we suggest in the introduction, to widen the perspective from which students look at the data they
have gathered and the questions they have raised. Whether the students have
explored a major, a broader academic area, or the school as a whole, these readings
will set their observations into a larger context and encourage them to ask more
wide ranging questions of their research.

Vocationalism and the Curriculum (p. 784)

Michael Moffatt

If your students have included interviews with other students in their research,
it should be interesting for them to set their findings next to Moffatt's and to
think about the similarities and differences. Even if they have not, it might make
an interesting mini-research project to poll your own class and then ask them
to poll friends and acquaintances, using Moffatt's questions, before they even
read this article. Did others — and do they — also classify subjects into "useful"
and "useless"? What makes the difference? What are the most popular majors
in your school? Do students' perceptions about academic disciplines parallel
faculty ideas? How might they find out? How is the status of a major determined?
If students have friends in other schools, they might inquire about the relative
status of majors in other places. Is there some uniformity from one school to
another, or are there vast differences? What seems to determine this kind of status?
Question 4, about the discourse of the major, should make for some interesting
discussion, especially if students have been considering language issues during
their own research. You might also want to talk with students about the values
implicit in Moffatt's findings — and about whether they and their friends share
those values. Do their professors? Does the catalogue? Do their parents? Can they
draw any conclusions about all this?

Gender, Language, and Pedagogy (p. 789)

Elizabeth Chiseri-Strater

How do your students respond to the distinctions Chiseri-Strater makes between
male discourse and female discourse? Do her statements ring true to their own
experience and to what they have observed? If they're not sure, hold off on
conclusions for a while and suggest that they watch in their classes for a few
days and see what they observe. What implications might the differences have
for choice of a major, for preferred subjects, for favorite teachers, for learning
in general?

Do their observations confirm Chiseri-Strater's assertion that "the university
as an institution primarily rewards mastery or what Nick calls 'abbreviated
learning'"? Is the answer to that question different for different kinds and/or
sizes of schools?

Ask students to look again at the descriptions of classes in this article. Have
they experienced some of these different styles of teaching in their classes? How

do they respond? And how can language be used "as a weapon rather than a tool for constructing understandings"?

What do students think of the author's "solutions"? Have they had opportunities to "reflect on, revise, rethink, and personally construct what they are learning in one course and connect it to other courses and finally to themselves"? Do they see this as a worthwhile goal of education? Does their research confirm the problems and/or the solutions Chiseri-Strater discusses?

If You Want to Be a Scholar (p. 792)

Howard S. Becker

Becker's article should be an interesting counterpoint to students' research into the discourse of their major. What does Becker try to tell his student about the specialized language of the discipline? Why does she resist his advice? Is she right; is he wrong? The distinction between what he says and her idea that the jargon is "classier" may be reflected in students' research into the language of the major they are exploring. How would they characterize the language of the scholarly journals in their field? What did they find when they attended upper level lectures?

Becker connects language to the political hierarchy of the university. How? What is the student's attitude toward the discourse of the classroom and the journal? Why the unwillingness to question and the determination to imitate? How does Becker respond to and feel about Rosanna's attitude? Does this essay reflect or contradict what students have discovered about the existence of discourse communities within the university and outside it — or is the issue not so simple and have students discovered contradictory things?

Academic Discourse: Community or Communities? (p. 795)

David R. Russell

What differences does David Russell point out between the colleges of the past and the modern university? You might look with your students at the differences in who attends these schools, what roles they are expected to play in society, who teaches them and how (it's interesting to note where the instructional methods came from: German schools and scientific management). If you or your students have access to very old college catalogues, try to make some comparisons with recent catalogues to see how they support (or don't) Russell's assertions. How has the notion of community changed over time? Does the research of your students speak to Russell's description of the modern university as "tightly knit, turf-conscious disciplines and departments, each of its own discourse community"? One way to approach this question might be to form groups consisting of students who have investigated different majors and to ask them to share their observations. Russell also suggests that the disciplines are "bound up with professional communities outside academia." How does this idea fit with what your students have found? Have they investigated any of those outside communities? In what way(s) are they or are they not connected to the university disciplines?

Tyrannical Machines (p. 797)

Lynne V. Cheney

The tension between research and teaching is a familiar subject among professors, though it may be less so among students. You might bring in recent issues of academic publications or national newspapers that highlight the debate about which should be primary in higher education. How do students respond to the debate — and to the assertion in this article that research is more important than teaching to promotion and tenure in colleges and universities? How do money and status become related issues? Cheney describes as the "tyrannical machine" the model of the university that emphasizes "the production of knowledge rather than its diffusion." Is "diffusion" a powerful way to think about student learning? Might "construction" of knowledge be a more effective model for student learning? What do students think? What does Cheney think? How do students understand that phrase? In their research, have they found the distinction Cheney makes between communication with students and communication among colleagues?

You and they may notice that Cheney, like Russell, points to the acquisition of that model from the German system at the end of the nineteenth century. If any of your students is interested, a brief research foray into German education might be enlightening: What was the German system and why was it adopted here?

The role of the community colleges in the higher education system may be of interest to students who have attended local colleges. You might ask them to talk about their experiences: Do they see support for Cheney's statements in their own experience, and do they see the difference she describes between the community college and a four-year institution, if that is what they're now attending?

If your students are considering discourse communities as part of their own research, how do the views of discourse communities presented in these essays illuminate their understanding of what they have found?

The Enriched Major (p. 800)

Ernest Boyer

After looking at the larger context of American education past and present, students should find Boyer's findings directly relevant to their own research. Did they find the emphasis on careerism he describes? How do they view your school's general education requirements — if, indeed, the school has any? How does the *school* view them? It might be interesting to compare student perceptions, faculty perceptions, and the catalogue description of these requirements. You might even ask a dean or someone else who is responsible for curriculum to speak to the class about the rationale behind and the success of general requirements. In many schools, these requirements have changed over time; the historical perspective in your school should be interesting to consider.

It's also interesting to think about how new majors come to be within your school. Is the process and are the issues the same as what Boyer describes? And how does the research your students have done fit with Boyer's notion that "the basic test of a proposed major is this: Does the field of study have a legitimate intellectual content of its own and does it have the capacity to enlarge rather than narrow the vision of the student? Do the majors they have investigated meet these criteria?

How do they understand and respond to the idea of an enriched major? Does your school offer anything similar: Do some or all majors require that students respond to the questions Boyer poses? They might start by looking at the catalogue and the statements of the departments and then look at what students and faculty have said about each major. Are there differences, or are all majors similar in this way?

Rethinking the Cultures of Disciplines (p. 803)

Raymond J. Rodriques

To help students get an idea of the scope of the issues Rodrigues raises, you might direct their attention to debates in national newspapers, academic publications, and, perhaps, within your own school, about the proper content of the curriculum. Rodrigues suggests that curricula should respond to the changes in the student body and points out that the traditional disciplines are culture bound. Do students see evidence of this in their research? Do they see evidence of interdisciplinary approaches within their majors? Are certain methods of instruction common within each major area, or does method vary with individual instructor? What does Rodrigues mean by "culture," what does he see as cultural limitations, and how would he like to define academic discourse? Does your research suggest that his criticisms are valid; that his recommendations are important?

Options

The questions posed here ask students to look in a variety of ways at the data they have gathered and discussed and analyzed and at the reading they've done. Before they select an option for a longer piece of writing, you might ask for a short, exploratory piece that looks at the issues raised in the readings as they are reflected in or contradicted by the data gathered in the students' research.

The Options offer a wide range of approaches for individual or small group work. In addition to writing a substantial essay (or instead of it) students might organize and present a research forum for the class or for another group of students and/or faculty to share what they've learned. They might organize groups around particular options or they might adapt the questions posed here to their own research interests. Writing is an important part of the process, certainly. But this material offers an opportunity for discussion and presentation as well. At the end, you might even gather the papers into a document that resembles proceedings of a conference and duplicate it for all class members (an ambitious project, but probably worthwhile if time and funds permit).

Whatever you decide to do as the culminating project of the chapter, consider allowing some time for students to reflect (in their journals, perhaps) about what they have learned, about their understanding of discourse communities and particular kinds of academic communication, about how their research has or has not influenced their choice of major and their understanding of the workings of this particular school and American higher education in general.